WHERE ARE YOU GOING?

A Sales, Marketing, and Life Guide for an Entrepreneur

Lou Vickery

Jim (Gymbeaux) Brown

Copyright©2025

by Upword Press, LLC.

ISBN: 978-0-9654140-4-3

Upwordpress6@gmail.com

https://awiseword.life/library

www.youtube.com/@awiseword

Cover Design: Shannon Castello

OTHER BOOKS BY LOU
STILL IN PRINT

A TOUCH OF GRAY...Upword Press, LLC, 2001, 2016

**THE RISE OF THE POARCH BAND OF CREEK INDIANS,
Upword Press, LLC. 2009**

**THE LAUGH, GIGGLE, GRIN, AND THINK BOOK
Upword Press, LLC, 2010**

**NOTES FROM GOD
Upword Press, LLC 2011**

**GOOD STUFF FOR THE JOURNEY...
Upword Press, LLC, 2012**

**REACH BEYOND...Find Your Path to Success
Indigo Publishing, Inc. 2020**

**ALABAMA CREEK INDIANS...
Upword Press, LLC 2021**

**WINNING THE HEAD GAME...
Key to Athletic Success
-Upword Press, LLC 2021**

**HELLO! LET'S TALK!!
Upword Press, LLC 2023**

**WHAT'S YOUR RACKET?
Upword Press, LLC 2024**

For Details: www.awiseword.life/library

Also available at Amazon.com

Upwordpress6@gmail.com

ACCLAIM FOR...
WHERE ARE YOU GOING?

"**WHERE ARE YOU GOING? A Sales, Marketing, and Life Guide for an Entrepreneur is** a well-thought-out game plan by gifted authors and experienced coaches who have genuinely been through it themselves in multiple careers. The authors gained knowledge, delivered it experientially, succeeded famously, and now show you "how to" generate more success. It makes your journey more meaningful, profitable, and enjoyable! Learn from the best; grab a copy of this book."

-Doug Giesler, Best Selling Author, Life Coach, SC

"Informative, instructional, insightful, and inspiring! **WHERE ARE YOU GOING? Sales and Marketing Skills for an Entrepreneur** lays it all out, from the mindset to the logistics of what you need to create success in the sales and marketing arm of your entrepreneurial journey. In an easy-to-digest format, the authors' guidance is well thought out and comprehensive. A must-read, especially for entrepreneurs who need to upgrade their sales and marketing side of their business.

Yarona Boster, Owner & CEO –
Footprints Coaching LLC & Yarona Boster LLC. NJ

"I have known Lou for more than 40 years and he is "always" upbeat, positive, and on to the next challenge (or as Lou would say "the next batter") regardless of how difficult the path might appear to be which is the sign of a true entrepreneur. You must be "fearless" and able to absorb the risks involved with every challenge. I know this book will be a success and, because it is Lou, it has a definite "sales" emphasis throughout which has been Lou's calling. I'm honored to endorse not only the book, but also the man behind it.

Robert Taylor, CEO –
TayGroup Solutions Inc – Serial Entrepreneur, GA

I have known Jim Brown for over ten years. I happily call him a friend and confidante. Jim and Lou Vickery excellently wrote this book. Both men have used their extensive knowledge and experience to write a genuinely outstanding guidebook for all serious sales professionals. I read through the manuscript three times, taking notes on each occasion. It truly is compelling reading for any sales professional. The advice is easy to understand and cuts through much of the mystique and double-speak often found in sales books. If you are serious about a successful future as an entrepreneur, do yourself a favor and keep this book as your go-to reference—it will become an indispensable tool for you.

Kieran Revell International Leadership and Communication Consultant, Speaker, and Published Author, Australia

"This book goes well beyond sales and marketing—it's a blueprint for entrepreneurial success. **WHERE ARE YOU GOING? A Sales, Marketing, and Life Guide for an Entrepreneur** reveals what it truly takes to thrive in business. Lou and Jim embody their principles, offering an optimistic and practical guide that lays a strong foundation for what truly matters in business, sales, and lasting success. With real-world wisdom and actionable strategies, this book is full of gold. Apply the strategies in the book, and your entrepreneurial success isn't just possible—it's inevitable."

Dr. Laurel Mines, PT, DPT, OCS Bay Laurel Athletics Owner, Stanford University Teaching Specialist, CA

"If you are searching for a bridge to greater results in your journey to be the best you can be, the book **WHERE ARE YOU GOING? A Sales, Marketing, and Life Guide for an Entrepreneur** is a must-read. It is a path to follow as one searches for ways and means to reach their target goals. The book will provide you with insights and ideas that will motivate you to achieve the best results. Order your copy today.

-William Scruggs, Retired, Office of the District Attorney, MS.

"Do YOU know where you are going? Do you know how to get from here to there? How will you know when you get there? These are just some of the questions answered by the brilliant Lou Vickery and his writing partner, Jim Brown, in this monumental manuscript. Sales and marketing are essential components for a successful company. **WHERE ARE YOU GOING?** A **Sales, Marketing, and Life Guide for an Entrepreneur** is a concise database on how to succeed using effective sales and marketing tools and applications. I highly recommend this book."

Dt. Ted Broer, CEO of Healthmasters, Inc., FL

"**WHERE ARE YOU GOING? Sales, Marketing, and Life Guide for an Entrepreneur** is the ultimate spark for anyone needing direction or motivation. Whether you're a first-time entrepreneur seeking startup insights and the must-have basics for success or an experienced business owner looking to refresh your perspective with sales and marketing strategies and reminders, this book is packed with valuable insights, guidance, and motivation. It will empower entrepreneurs at any stage to push past their limits, navigate challenges, and seize opportunities that will elevate their careers and drive lasting success."

- Kris Bishop Fintech startup entrepreneur, CEO FIntegrate Tech.

An absolute must-read for any entrepreneur looking to elevate their Sales and Marketing game! This book simplifies the process by offering straightforward, actionable advice that is easy to understand and implement. With clear examples and real-life stories, the authors bring theory to life, demonstrating how to apply strategies and why they are effective. It's a refreshing approach that will empower you to make smarter, more confident decisions in your business. Whether you're just starting or looking to refine your strategy, this book will become your go-to guide for Sales and Marketing success!"

Mitch Carlson, COO, Business Information Solutions, AL

"If you're looking for inspiration and practical wisdom to propel your entrepreneurial journey forward, this book delivers! It challenges you to embrace your past, learn from it, and use it as fuel to create a more prosperous future. It's a roadmap to growth, offering new perspectives and empowering insights to help you achieve the success you've been striving for. It is highly recommended for anyone ready to level up!"
-Steve Means, Real Estate Executive, AL

The one word I would use to describe **WHERE ARE YOU GOING? Sales, Marketing, and Life Guide for an Entrepreneur** is illuminating! As one reads this book from cover to cover, numerous valuable insights can be gained. It outlines valuable keys to successful sales, marketing, and career life. I highly recommend this insightful book to entrepreneurs, or anyone interested in becoming an entrepreneur; it will leave you feeling like a winner!
-LaTonya C. Prim, RN, MSN, CRNP, AL, FL

"This powerful book offers a straightforward, no-nonsense guide to mastering the sales and marketing skills every entrepreneur needs but few naturally possess. Whether transitioning from a successful career within a company (as an intrapreneur) or launching your first business, this book shows you why sales and marketing are the lifeblood of entrepreneurship—and how to excel in them. At its core, the book emphasizes that no matter how great your product, idea, or service is, success hinges on your ability to communicate its value and connect with customers. The authors walk readers through identifying their ideal customers, crafting a compelling message, and building a consistent, recognizable brand. They also cover practical strategies: building email lists, creating effective landing pages, leveraging lead magnets, and making your follow-up process genuine."
David Chametzky, Podcast Host, Speaker. Author, NY

"**WHERE ARE YOU GOING? A Sales, Marketing, and Life Guide for an Entrepreneur** is a guidepost for anyone seeking transformation in their entrepreneurial journey. It provides a clear path from where you are now to where you want to be, offering fresh perspectives and actionable insights. Written in an accessible and engaging style, this book simplifies complex ideas, making it an invaluable resource for both new and seasoned entrepreneurs. A must-read for those ready to take their business and mindset to the next level!"

-Jeff Vaage, Life Coach, IA

"Lou is an amazing talent, both on and off the business field! His insights in **WHERE ARE YOU GOING? A Sales, Marketing, and Life Guide for an Entrepreneur** is foundational. It is a must-read for aspiring entrepreneurs and seasoned professionals looking to up their sales and marketing game!

-Jacob Clendenning, TV Host, Executive Coach, WY

"A real estate broker for 45+ years who finally graduated from the school of hard knocks, I sure wish I had read Lou and Jim's book at the beginning of my career! The lessons taught here are so true. The best chapter, Fail Forward, is spot on."

T. Nicholas Gill, H.A. Gill and Sons,
Real Estate, DC

"**Where Are You Going? A Sales, Marketing, and Life Guide for an Entrepreneur** was a compelling and enjoyable read from start to finish. Lou shares his wisdom earned from a lifetime of studying and striving for constant self-improvement. This book provides not only sound advice for those seeking to elevate their abilities to a higher, more focused level, but it is also full of fundamental life lessons that apply to all of us."

Mike Vincent, President and CEO
of United Bank, AL and FL

"This is a very practical guide in all aspects of life, including sales and marketing. I enjoyed the focus on emotional intelligence. Being called a person with a high EQ was never something I learned until later in life. Jim Fortin is known for saying that the greatest cause of human suffering is when we hold onto expectations of others and outcomes. The only thing we can control is ourselves. Lou and Jim touch on this masterfully throughout the book. This book is a simple yet profound guide to mastering the art of communication and navigating the full range of human emotions, while always finding joy in the moments."

Lisa J. Wood, Owner + Principal Designer, Speaker , NC

" What is the legacy you wish to leave? What impact do you hope to make? With the wisdom contained in this book, you will find the tools to design a life of meaning and achievement that contributes to the greater good. Lou and Jim remind us that success is not a matter of chance, but rather a matter of choice. It results from deliberate action, guided by purpose and fueled by desire and determination."

Randy Burgan, Syndicated Radio Show Host, AL.FL, MS

"Let me ask you something: Are you spinning your wheels, stuck doing the same thing over and over, but expecting a different result? You're not alone—it's the hallmark of madness! But you don't have to settle for that. Oh no, you don't. Here's the deal: Lou Vickery and Jim Brown, two extraordinary thinkers, have mapped out the ultimate blueprint for breaking free and building something greater—something more meaningful than you have ever experienced. Their book, **'Where Are You Going? A Sales, Marketing, and Life Guide for an Entrepreneur'** is not just a guide; it's a declaration of freedom for the entrepreneurial spirit. You'll get all the tools you need to design a business and a life filled with purpose and triumph."

-Jerry Williams, Entrepreneur Retired, Living the Good Life.

Where're You Going?

High in the Sierra Mountains lives an old man
Who, from their hermitage, looks down in pity
Upon other people of higher mental aspiration.

One day he rescued a little group of Swiss mountaineers
Lost deep in the mountains' fastnesses.
When told where they were, they exclaimed in disbelief,
"But how did we get here?"

To which the old hermit replied,
"If that question ain't got no answer attached to it,
I ain't got none that fits.
If you is goin' anywhere in particular
Up here, yu'd better figger fust how to get thar.
Cuz by jest goin' afore ya know where yere agoin'
Ya can get to a powerful lotta places ya might
not wanta be."
　　　　　　　　-Author unknown

Do YOU know where you are going?

Do you know how to get from here to there?

How will you know when you get there?

Read on!

CONTENTS

PROLOGUE

<u>Elevation of your dreams</u>

<u>Elevation of your best sales and marketing skills</u>

<u>Elevation of your effort with every customer</u>

<u>Elevation of your life results</u>

We are excited that you have chosen to read *"WHERE ARE YOU GOING? A Sales, Marketing, and Life Guide for an Entrepreneur."* Whatever connected us, we are thankful we can share this time.

What qualifies us to write such a book? We have over 70 years of sales and marketing experience, which provides a background that brings the content of this book to life. We do not write from theory; we have been in the arena.

What mission do we want to accomplish in *"WHERE ARE YOU GOING? A Sales, Marketing, and Life Guide for an Entrepreneur."* It's to apply our expertise and experience to create a deep desire in you to explore and expand your sales and marketing capabilities. We want to help you become the entrepreneur you may have only dreamed of becoming.

We didn't write the book based on their present status and boundaries. We sense that you have something unfinished by being here—something you believe can be much more significant in your entrepreneurial journey. Sales and marketing are developmental processes. Our purpose is to help you move from potential to reality. Our mission is to provide the ingredients to help you build a bridge from where you are to where you want to be.

BUT NOW

The entrepreneurial world is full of former highly successful intrapreneurial businesspeople who brought that mindset into their entrepreneurial careers. They know what it takes to be successful because they have created great performance habits, and applying those habits to their work as entrepreneurs is just a natural step.

However, sales and marketing are areas in which many highly qualified entrepreneurs fall short of their capabilities. If we were to assign a label to your current marketing ability, what would it indicate? Here is what we often hear from aspiring entrepreneurs: *"I'm not a salesperson,"* or *"I've never sold anything before."*

One thing is sure: You cannot afford to *"just get by"* if you want to be highly successful in your entrepreneurial journey. Is there any question that you are reading this book to improve your sales and marketing capabilities?

Here's our preview of the entrepreneurial sales and marketing journey. Initially, you must be as specific as possible in determining who your product or service is genuinely intended for. It is one thing to have a dream and another to know how to market it. Who are the people who are ready to buy your dream? Where are they located? What is your plan to capture them?

Establishing your brand, which conveys a strategic, consistent, and clear message about your company, is essential. Develop a powerful brand that helps accelerate your impact in the marketplace.

Do you have a hook? What is the result of someone buying what you are proposing and doing everything you say? What is the gateway challenge you will help them solve? What ambition are you helping them achieve? Set the hook to make the big catch.

Okay. You have your hook established. What next? You now employ every avenue possible, from word of mouth to paid ads, to get your message in the mix. You are very good at what you do, but getting your business off the ground or moving in the right direction requires a definitive plan for locating and gathering probable customers.

FREE. This word is a lead magnet. What do you have that offers value you can give away for free? Use your imagination here. We will have more on a FREE giveaway later in the chapter on Locating and Gathering Leads.

What does your website look like? An attractive landing page is essential in today's digital landscape. It doesn't have to be elaborate. It has to be explicit and straightforward. It should be a view of who you are and what you offer to probable buyers.

How many people are on your potential customer list? You are not interested in just anyone but in those who will be your ideal customer. If you were asked, do you have the names of your top ten prospects earmarked for today?

Engage your prospective customers with content regularly. Contact all previous customers. Follow up. Follow up. Then, follow up some more. How long do you follow up? Until they tell you "Yes" or "No," if they are in the market to buy. What you are looking for from your present customers is referrals.

Locate and gather new contacts and develop a detailed list of their email addresses and phone numbers. Give your business card to anyone you meet who you think is a prospect. Utilize software programs to assist in locating customers (more details to follow). Develop an elevator pitch of about 30 seconds to deliver to a probable prospect.

A lot needs to be done to elevate your capabilities to match the level of your entrepreneurial dream. We have skimmed the surface of the steps to be taken. But you will find the details as you move through the book.

Treat this book as a resource book. Keep it readily available for reference regularly. Maximize its use.

Where you are in your entrepreneurial journey matters, but the unseen qualities, abilities, and possibilities that lie ahead are more critical. This book is about growing your business through enhanced sales and marketing, including promotional skills. You may not have world-class sales talent—very few do—but you can substantially elevate what you have.

The words in this book have little meaning unless they inspire you to become a better version of yourself. Our role is to provide high-quality information that helps you transition from developing your sales and marketing skills to achieving your full potential in your entrepreneurial career.

We encourage you to do something that moves you. Don't think about it. Don't just talk about it. Lay out your plans for it and then act on them. Let go and see what happens. Your purpose is the fuel that keeps your desire strong and gives you the inner drive to improve.

Here's an essential point that we don't want you to miss. If you consistently put in extra work to refine your sales and marketing skills, you will develop the skill level necessary to succeed at a championship level. This attitude may not always make you better, but we guarantee it won't make you worse.

With this *"do a little bit more"* attitude, you get up every day with a desire to improve. It becomes a habit. It becomes a part of you. It's no longer something you do…it's who you are.

Generating entrepreneurial salesmanship is about building momentum. Get on a roll. Have some success every day. The most sacred thing that you can give to your business is *effort.*

The most excellent sales and marketing tool you have is the combination of determination and effort. A merger of these two will develop momentum, creating a solid path to fulfilling your entrepreneurial dreams. We will talk about these two in more depth later in the book. However, for now, let's focus on what is needed to jump-start your entrepreneurial career.

YOU ARE A MESSENGER

The centerpiece of sales and marketing is first to understand that you are a messenger. We have already concluded that you are an exceptionally talented person with a fantastic idea that will significantly enhance your clients' lives. But how do you find a way to bridge the gap between your present clients and the unfulfilled ones waiting to hear your message?

The honest answer is found in the authentic role you will play, in your ability to add value to the lives of more customers and convert them into clients. A customer is a number on the stat sheet unless you offer a one-time product for sale. A client is someone with whom you establish a professional relationship, and they consistently purchase from you.

When value is created, you resonate with a potential customer, leading to a greater purpose beyond products and services. When customers perceive you as a messenger who conveys information that adds value to their lives, they increase their trust in you, your company, and your products and services. This broader message is what turns customers into clients. Then, they would not think of failing to give you the first shot at their future business…and will send you referrals.

There is no question that behind the messenger concept is your desire to develop more clients by making the message you bring to them more meaningful. The point is that the more powerful your ability to communicate value to your customers, the greater your chance to monetize both current and future-oriented efforts with your customers and potential clients.

To influence others as a messenger, we suggest that you employ these personal affirmations:

- **I have a** mission-oriented sales and marketing program that will leave a lasting legacy beyond my own.
- **I have a** passion-driven desire that will serve as a

guiding light for pursuing sales aggressively.

- **I have a** sense of purpose, where I see my primary role as being crucial in the lives of my customers and clients.

- **I employ a focused approach to identifying and generating** new leads. I do not go to work; my work is wherever I can locate and gather new customers.

- **I have a** well-thought-out proposal that aligns the presentation of my products' and services' features and benefits.

- **I have a** unique desire to learn and apply methods that help me get a "Yes" from my potential customers

- **I have a** sense of anticipation. I often anticipate the objections potential customers may raise before they are actually raised.

- **I have an** understanding of the importance of following up with potential customers who have not purchased.

- **I have a** sense of urgency that service to my customers is a product.

- **I have a** desire to ensure that I do all I am capable of doing to convert customers into clients.

When you tune yourself into a foundational base where a room full of possibilities exists, you have no idea what awaits you in this new paradigm. You might realize and appreciate for the first time that your unique sales and marketing personality is just waiting for you to discover it. You may not know what lies ahead when you unlock your natural gifts, but when you do, you will excel. You will be so thrilled with the possibilities offered by a new you, that you will burst at the seams to get started. Are you up to the task?

Chapter One

FROM HERE TO THERE

Where are you headed with your entrepreneurial career? Do you know what it will take to get from where you are to where you want to be? What is your current sales and marketing performance like? Are you doing okay, pretty good, or not good at all? We have already distinguished one area of your entrepreneurial business where you cannot afford to *"just get by,"* if you want to be an elite entrepreneur. That area requires superb sales and marketing skills. Marketing encompasses promotions and advertising.

What is essential to being highly effective in selling is to leave yourself some wiggle room for alterations. A critical factor in determining the level of effectiveness you experience is making quality adjustments on your entrepreneurial journey. This creates a need to make changes when needed. It is sometimes necessary to reassess your approach to be more effective.

Our experience has shown that many more experienced entrepreneurs remain tied to outdated trappings. They forego something better at the expense of continuing along the same old, comfortable path, doing things the same old convenient way, and end up with the same old results.

Do you find yourself in a *"sea of sameness*?" To escape the *"sea of sameness,"* do you know what sets you apart from others attempting to achieve the same goals? Do you know what your *"points of difference"* are? If you don't, you will be no more than just one of the hundreds, if not thousands, of people attempting to make the same or similar sale, accomplish the same goal, and achieve the same degree of success. Want to be different? What you will find in this book are ideas that will make you and what you provide different from the others.

Consider driving a vehicle. One of the first things you learn is to stay in your lane. Today's new vehicles are equipped with "lane departure" software that alerts you when you are moving outside your designated lane. If we, as entrepreneurs, only had such a device to help us know when we venture outside our lanes.

Each vehicle is also equipped with an "age-old" device called the *turn signal.* We are supposed to use it every time we change lanes. This means we give our full attention to a new path we must take. Then, to let everyone know, including your subconscious mind, using your turn signal permits you to make that change.

Changing lanes might mean expanding your business or modifying the services or products you offer, all of which can positively impact the people you aim to serve. Is it time to consider changing lanes and exploring new and more effective sales tactics and marketing methods? Learning, redirection, and adjusting are key elements in your growth as an entrepreneur.

We feel you would not be here unless you welcome and even accept the need for sales and marketing alterations. Your thought pattern toward sales and marketing cannot be static if you want to reach goals that stretch your limits. Reaching the pinnacle of effectiveness requires applying the impeccable ideas presented in these pages to your sales and marketing efforts.

There comes a time when a genuine commitment to doing something different is necessary to experience something truly unique. That is the first phase in developing a comprehensive change strategy. The energy to pursue something different with vigor and excitement lies within the consciousness of envisioning how that "something" will ultimately get you from here to there. The whole concept of where are you going, depends on it.

But let us offer a word of caution: Be very deliberate in examining your current level of effectiveness. Your current skills may need a little fine-tuning, rather than a complete overhaul. You can take as much or as little as you like from what we offer here. If you determine that something is not working as well as you want it, or as it once did, then focus on the necessary changes.

The type and size of the changes you wish to make are based solely on what you need to do to move from one point to another. The consequences of your choices will either clarify your commitments toward what you have been doing or lead you to make new decisions that will enable you to perform at a higher level. The choice is yours.

The next phase is to establish clear goals and objectives for improving your sales efficiency in the future. If your marketing actions are not generating the desired success, the focus moves to what does? Concentrate on expanding your skill set with the excellent tools you will experience in this book. Then, apply them to enhance your overall effectiveness, which in turn leads to future growth. Be flexible and mobile in your thinking process.

The questions before you are as follows: What am I willing to do differently to be more effective? Am I willing to step out of my comfort zone and expand my skills? Am I ready to explore new ways of performing and even venture into something unknown? Am I prepared to reach beyond and grasp something that has not been a part of my daily routine? Am I ready to apply my learning to ways that improve myself?

The last phase in an improvement plan is the action phase. The difference-maker is to ensure, through redirection, that you are headed in the right direction. As the book title indicates, you may not always know where you are going. But as the poem entitled *"Where're Going?"* shows, it will serve you well to have a good sense of the direction you want to take before you start. Our goal is to help you get there.

Change works best when there is a sustained effort to focus on what will make you more effective. Our focus here is to be a conduit of information, you spend time studying and digesting things that will improve your sales and marketing skills. Applying these newfound skills requires maximum attention as you put them into practice. This will eventually bring to fruition the new constructive thinking you have employed in your daily entrepreneurial sales efforts.

Set up a preparation course to enhance your effectiveness — and, consequently, your results. Review the Table of Contents and determine which direction of study you need to engage in first. Again, it's your choice where you begin and at the pace you travel.

> The significant change in your journey you've been wanting to make... make it now. Get a running start and jump right in —and you might just be surprised at the stunning and exciting place you land.

CHANGE...CHANGES

Here are some personalized reminders as you embark on upgrading your entrepreneurial sales and marketing:

- **I will** learn to live with what I cannot change... and change those things I can change.

- **I will** realize whatever got me to where I am today won't be good enough to keep me there tomorrow.

- **I will** recognize that doing what I have always done won't get the same results I have always gotten.

- **I will** do what I have never done to have a chance to receive what I have never had.

- **I will** do things I dislike to bring about things I do like.

- **I will** appreciate having something different; I must do something different...daily.

Chapter Two

ATTITUDE IS EVERYTHING

Dallas, Texas, 1986. I (Lou)had the opportunity to be on the speaking program with the legendary Zig Ziglar. I did my ten-minute gig and looked forward to hearing Zig speak.

When he arrived on the stage, Zig first surveyed the crowd, saying nothing. It seemed like five minutes, but it was only a few seconds. Then he spoke: *"Attitude is everything!"* He paused again, surveying the crowd for a second time.

In this moment of silence, the thoughts of others were likely similar to mine. The word "Everything" circled my brain like a big question mark. Really? I thought as Zig continued. *"Yes, everything we think, every decision we make, and every course of action we take is influenced, either directly or indirectly, by our attitude. We are our attitudes, and our attitudes are us."*

Nothing has been written about, talked about, or discussed more than the importance of success in anything than this mental state called *attitude.* *"Okay,"* you might ask, *"I see that this attitude thing is important, but what exactly is an attitude?"* We define attitude as a predisposition to think positively or negatively about the circumstances, events, situations, and people encountered daily.

After making these decisions over time, deciding how to react to the same stimuli in your environment takes little conscious effort. In essence, you have created a habit. Initially, you form your attitudes, and those same attitudes lead to the development of habits. Both your attitudes and habits shape who you become.

You can take this to the bank; sales and marketing success begins with your overall attitude, with what's inside you, not what's around you. Please pay close attention to your attitude, as it is a critical factor in your entrepreneurial journey, because your attitude will often determine the outcomes of most things that happen to you.

One fascinating aspect of the right mindset is that you consistently view any situation from a positive perspective. While you cannot control everything that happens to you, you can face what happens with a positive mindset. With this mindset, things improve because you do everything possible to enhance them. You learn to adjust your attitude to be more positive. You find yourself doing things to make the best of what's less than ideal.

This is big. When you approach your decisions and choices with an affirmative frame of mind, the force of this mindset moves you toward rather than moving away, embracing rather than rejecting, the challenges before you. I guarantee that you cannot think of negative thoughts and expect positive answers.

Do you need to overcome specific negative thought patterns? Making a sustained effort to change external behavior has, as its beginning, changed underlying internal attitudes and feelings. When positive behavior is the centerpiece of your daily activities, you will eventually bring about genuine external change.

Your positive mindset will beget a positive response to outside stimuli. You will see things differently and react to them differently. This might be the most critical effort you ever make in your life. This effort is designed to act on your behalf and enhance your results.

Your trademark should be a stable, consistent, positive state of mind that remains constructive despite ups and downs and varied fluctuations. The way you behave, think, and feel is learned behavior. Being mindful of this should make you more vigilant in suspending negative thoughts and pessimistic reactions. This creates a perspective for something good to happen regularly.

Whatever steps, however small, you take towards learning to reduce the influence of negative attitudes will make a difference in everything you do. To right the ship may take a while. Negative thoughts will occasionally arise, but you can choose how to respond to them.

Therefore, managing the negativity that arises from certain activities and events in your sales life is the first step toward addressing them more optimistically. Take a cue from the movie-makers and "*Take two*" when those negative thoughts pop up. Replace that negative thought with a positive, uplifting view.

Studies show that people with optimistic thinking habits experience more quality benefits than their pessimistic counterparts. They are healthier, have more energy, make better decisions, perform better, are less stressed, and are more productive overall than pessimists. It's worth thinking about.

POSITIVITY: THE FOUNDATION

Little can stop you with the right attitude,
little can help you with the wrong attitude.

Positivity serves as the foundation for building a bright future. It is needed as an entrepreneur because you constantly face an intriguing list of demanding challenges. Converting your desire to be a superb entrepreneur into reality depends significantly on how you employ positive thinking habits. For better or worse, these habits have contributed to your current level of performance and will continue to be the driving force behind your future level of performance.

Numerous misunderstandings have been raised regarding the creation and maintenance of positive thinking habits. It takes much more than repeating many feel-good one-liners (even though they help) to make positive thinking work in your life. It takes a solid understanding of what being positive means. It is being consciously aware, moment by moment, to focus on creating a positive mindset.

Experts tell us that over 50,000 thoughts pass through our minds daily, but we can only think one at a time. The task before you every moment is to control that single thought. Think about something positive, not negative, about what is good with you and not bad, about what can go right and not wrong.

Be Positive

When positivity is your trademark, those around you will consistently be drawn to your optimistic attitude and enthusiastic behavior. The simplicity of thinking and acting positively demonstrates to them the joy of life that resides within you. Others will want to experience some of the same excitement that you possess. They will want some of the glow and warmth you bring to your daily activities. You don't need to wear a sign telling others how you feel on the inside. They see it. They sense it. They know it. They enjoy being in your presence…and you make the most of it.

POSITIVE CHANGE

We humans have the innate ability to adjust and change our thought patterns. You can learn to view events positively by regularly applying attentive presence and effort. This will eventually lead you to be pointed consistently toward the positive side. It will serve you excellently in a sales and marketing world that constantly presents complex challenges. It also allows you to mitigate the adverse challenges that arise in sales.

Your positive train of thought works best when you focus on the present moment. This attention helps you perform at a high level, regardless of how circumstances unfold.

Chapter Three

BELIEVE IN YOU

Am I where I am because that's where I want
to be? If I am not where I want to be, what
is keeping me from moving from where I am
to where I want to be? Could it possibly
be that I don't believe enough in me?
-An unknown young salesperson

Are you connected to the best you? Your most incredible value to your future as an entrepreneur will be how connected you are with the best you. The stronger the connection to yourself, the better the connection to your future. Wrap your hands around that bit of wisdom.

No matter how much or how little you have expanded. No matter how far you think you are from your goals, the power to move on, improve, master, and experience the exhilaration that comes from being top-notch in entrepreneurial sales depends substantially on how you feel about yourself. Can you picture that?

Your first goal is to come alive to the seeds of great potential within you. That's right: within you is all the potential you need to enhance your foundation and develop your sales and marketing skills. This potential may be immature and undeveloped, but it is there. With proper preparation and efficient application, your potential will grow and develop.

Your first step is to consciously create a mental picture of how the precepts you read here will feel once achieved. See yourself applying these great sales and marketing lessons—if they resonate with you. Hear those around you congratulate you on your improvement. Visualize the desired result. See yourself stepping out and stepping up, refocusing beyond your current situation to seek new and greater possibilities in sales and life.

When the appropriate feelings and emotions come together, you will make great strides in those areas of your career you desire to improve. Armed with this energy and power, you will bring renewed substance to your daily affairs. But you must honestly believe in your heart that it will make a difference in the future.

"If you believe in yourself, have dedication and pride, and never quit, you'll be a winner. The price of victory is high – but so are the rewards."
-Paul (Bear) Bryant

SELF-CONNECTION

Do you understand that self-connection fosters the confidence necessary to bring a higher value to your external relationships? You interact with others on a higher level when you feel truly confident in who you are and what they gain from you.

What would it take to help undo the layers of inadequate thoughts and emotions that may hinder your ability to form a better connection with yourself? Would you not think that if you honor yourself more positively, your actual value will show in how you approach people and the openness with which they approach you?

The more you value yourself, the more valuable you become to yourself and others. Consider this: as you increase your appreciation of your self-worth, you also enhance your ability to recognize and value others. Expanding your sales skills increases your value to your future customers.

This journey will not be easy. But with a forward-looking attitude, each step will count. You will grow closer and closer to being the salesperson you want to be. Please understand that the journey never ends. You always have plenty of work to do.

This journey requires constantly letting go of the antiquated to make room for something better. The more space you create for something better, the more you raise your status in the world around you. You will increase the depth and breadth of who you are because you will be a more skillful person. Doing things that enhance your value to yourself improves what you are doing to advance your career as an entrepreneur.

The vastness of the unknown, called the future, is looking for the very best you to tackle it. Being the best you is the key to unleashing your dreams, aspirations, and ambitions. Are you up to the task?

THE "RIGHT STUFF"

One of the most significant discoveries you can make is realizing that your talents and abilities will determine what you can physically accomplish. Your knowledge and skills will determine what you can do mentally. But your attitude toward yourself and your ability to perform will determine how well you do it.

Once you embrace who you are, you have positioned yourself to visualize the successful entrepreneur you can become realistically. Your mental process then flows in a constant state toward becoming that salesperson.

There is little doubt that many entrepreneurs who have gone on to greater heights have had to overcome self-doubt about themselves. Most likely, there were times when they wondered if they could meet and overcome all the challenges they would face as they traveled the path toward their sales goals.

But when they were not making progress, they took stock of themselves. They believed they had the right stuff to succeed in the entrepreneurial world. They believed that, despite setbacks and temporary feelings of doubt, the renewed positivity of their mindset would propel them toward more significant progress and vastly greater possibilities.

The top-level entrepreneurs recognized that the most important thing they had to work with was what they possessed from the bottom of their feet to the top of their heads. They had everything they needed within themselves, and it was up to them to ensure they never lost sight of that fact, even when faced with tough sledding.

Consider these words: Believing you have the "right stuff" will not automatically create new talents and abilities. This attitude toward yourself helps you release, utilize, and maximize your incredible talent and skills.

STATE OF BECOMING

We can say without reservation that top-level success as an entrepreneur begins inside of you, not around you. As an inside-out proposition, you cannot always change what goes on around you, but you can change your thoughts about what is happening around you.

You cannot always create a different kind of environment, but you can make the best of the domain you are in. We have probably already mentioned this, but we will repeat it with an emphasis on its importance: Make the best of what may be considered less than the best.

It starts with creating a mindset where things improve because you did something to improve them. You can invariably adjust your attitude to accommodate an environment favorable to improving yourself.

When you create a mental picture of success, you train your mind to work at what it takes to be successful. This begins with an internal set of expectations that you make every effort to function at a peak level, whatever the odds. Those expectations expand the ability to achieve on a higher plane.

If you want to become the salesperson you want to be but are not progressing as well as you would like, don't blame your shortcomings solely on talent and ability. How do you know the extent of your capabilities? You don't!

The barrier to becoming the best at entrepreneurial sales you can become has little to do with your capabilities. It depends on the application of all your faculties in building and developing the abilities you possess.

We are discussing that the fulfillment of your desires depends on releasing more and more of the undiscovered potential locked within you. It is there, and your ability to unfold this potential is always in a state of becoming.

Visualize the entrepreneur you can become, not the one you are. This will keep you from setting a limit on what you can achieve. From this starting point, work diligently every day to enhance your performance. No price is too great to pay. Remember: Make the most of who you are...for that is all there will ever be of you.

> *Out of all the possibilities available to you in any situation, you will select the one consistent with the performer you see yourself being. You will perform the way you believe you can. No more. No less!*

"EXCEPT FOR ME, THERE GOES I"

Numerous years ago, a noted cartoonist for the Disney Corporation took time from his busy schedule, drawing the "frames" for a new movie called "Hercules," to create a caricature of me (Lou) pitching a baseball. It became one of my most cherished possessions.

As a fan of caricatures, I (Lou) have collected many over the years. One that has stood out to me depicts a bum sitting on a park bench watching a chauffeured limousine ease by. The caption reads: "*Except for me, there goes I.*"

Those words mean so much because they are so true. They point the finger in the right direction. Who can we blame if we fail to fulfill our dreams and aspirations? Should we blame our failures on circumstances? Who creates the significant circumstances in which we find ourselves?

Who ultimately makes the choices that decide—even alter—who we are and where we are going? Can we place the blame on others? Do we honestly believe that other people have more influence over our decisions than we do? Or is the barrier to becoming the person we want to be the person looking back at us in the mirror? Aren't we the chief architects of how our lives turn out? Do you truly believe that?

Although your environment does play a role in achieving success, you do not have to be at the mercy of outside circumstances. On the contrary, you can deliberately choose how those events affect your life. Never lay the blame for your lack of progress solely on the conditions around you. Regardless of external influences, you hold the power to make the best of anything you are confronted with.

Those who have gone on to greater heights as entrepreneurs have had to overcome some self-doubt about themselves. At times, they may have wondered if they could meet all the new challenges they would face as they traveled along the road to sales success. But during these times of hesitation, they took stock of themselves. They worked hard to develop the belief that they had the right stuff to succeed in sales and marketing.

Despite setbacks or feelings of doubt, they possessed the mindset that propelled them toward more extraordinary things. Their mental fortitude assured them that everything they needed could be found within themselves, and they never lost sight of that, even when the going became difficult.

Where do you start in turning things around? When you point one finger at what you believe is the cause of your shortcomings, three fingers point back at you. Accepting responsibility for where you are, if you are not where you want to be, is the starting point for moving toward your desired destination. Once you recognize that something better starts with you, you have positioned yourself to visualize what needs to be done to become the entrepreneur you have dreamed of becoming.

Little change will occur if you continually focus only on your present state. If you routinely envision the salesperson you want to become, that's the direction you will take in your sales career. *Except for me, there goes I"* is a truism.

The portrait you paint of yourself is the single most telling factor in determining your success in any aspect of life.

You unfold your potential the best when you habitually think about the person you can become. Then you find yourself focusing on your strengths rather than your limitations...on why you can succeed...not on what might hold you back. It is true: When you begin to believe that you can be the successful salesperson your vision tells you can become, that's when you reach out toward the future and do things you have always dreamed of doing... things you possibly never thought you could do.

Ability is a gift and a challenge. It is something you use—not just something you have... and the more of your ability you use, the more you realize you have available to use.

Be a victor in the greatest competition of all –
the competition with yourself.

I AM...

-A Personal Affirmation-

I AM a more unique and special person than I have ever appreciated.

I AM far more talented and gifted as a person than I have ever dared to imagine.

I AM fully capable of growing beyond any performance level I have ever achieved.

I AM much stronger and more courageous than my inner fears have allowed me to be.

I AM far more competent in handling difficult situations than I have ever thought possible.

I AM able to generate more inner strength to handle tough setbacks and missteps than I have given myself credit for.

I AM more proficient and adept in satisfying my heart's desire than I have ever dreamed..

God richly endows me with the capabilities to move beyond what I am for the greater reward of what I can become.

I believe this with all my heart...because it is true.

Chapter Four

"GREAT TO MEET YOU"

This chapter has what we term *"Behind-the-curtain information."* It is the first step as you embark on the journey to convert a potential buyer into a confirmed buyer. The focus here is on the difference between being good or excellent in meeting potential customers. Your first impression is crucial.

Undoubtedly, some people have a greater receptivity to social interaction than others. Okay. Others around you may have a more natural, outgoing personality. Does that mean you shouldn't develop and grow your interpersonal relational skills?

We would be the first to admit that personality is vague and intangible. It may be reasonably challenging to explain, but not so difficult to recognize. The question comes up: Can one improve one's personality? Sure, they can.

Do I hear you asking, *"What can I do specifically to enhance my personality? How can I strengthen my ability to make a more lasting impression on the people I meet?*

INITIAL CONTACT

What do you want to accomplish during the initial contact phase? Here's the crux of your initial campaign:

- Lower defensive barriers.
- Create a receptive attitude.
- Establish rapport/show empathy.
- Build interest/develop trust.
- Establishing credentials and expertise.
- Create a successful image for your products/company.

YOUR FIRST STEP

Let's get specific. Before asking anyone to take action, you must overcome the natural barriers that probable customers face when they meet you for the first time. This holds true even for those you have known personally for years if this is their first time being exposed to your new opportunity.

Your primary priority is simple: lower the defensive barriers and anxiety levels that are generally the highest during the initial contact phase. What must you do to lower these defensive barriers?

First, let's examine why prospective clients create defensive barriers. This occurs primarily because of previous experiences with aggressive and thoughtless people trying to sell them things. Here are some of the most common concerns prospects have:

- Being taken advantage of.
- Being given the runaround.
- Being pressured to act.
- Insecure about finances.
- Not excited about making a buying decision.
- Worried they will receive unwanted contact if they give you their personal contact information.

There are potentially six questions on the mind of every new prospect that may create an element of anxiety. The number that may apply to each prospect will vary, but you must be prepared with a satisfying answer to each question:

- *"Can I trust what this person says?*
- *"Does this person know what they are talking about?"*
- *"Will this person listen to my point of view?"*
- *"Will this person answer my questions truthfully?*
- *"Will this person push me to buy?"*
- *"Will this person be more interested in what they can give me, rather than what they can get from me?"*

FIRST IMPRESSIONS

What is the 7/11 rule of first impressions? Research has shown that within the initial 7 seconds of meeting someone, they will have formed eleven impressions of you.

Prospects will notice your facial expressions, the clothes you wear and how you wear them, your height and how confidently you stand, how you carry yourself and your overall manner and bearing, your eye contact, your handshake, and the tone of your voice and voice confidence.

When dealing with the public, you can always expect to be under scrutiny. That microscope can reveal any faults and flaws you may possess. In those first seven seconds, the tone is set for the ultimate and ongoing success you experience when meeting someone for the first time. Right or wrong, fair or unfair, first impressions are vital to your success with someone you have just met. And just how many times do you get to make a favorable first impression?

Do you make a lasting, positive first impression? Nothing is more important in mounting a new relationship successfully than making a good initial impression. It sets the stage for all future interactions with this prospect.

Investing more time and effort to improve the ability to make a favorable first impression enhances that possibility. An excellent first impression creates a broader and more sustainable pattern of relationship building. You experience higher results— not only in terms of dollars and cents but also in terms of impact on your customers and fulfillment of their purchase purpose.

Maximizing your ability to make a great first impression aligns you with something secure with prospective clients. They sense the importance of your attentiveness to their needs and wants, as well as your desire to help them through the buying process. An excellent first impression pays many dividends

How many times do you get to make a great first impression?

APPROACHABILITY

The ability to make a favorable initial impression largely depends on your approachability. Approachability is best described as a unique appeal we possess that attracts others to us with ease and comfort.

Let's get specific. There is no hint of doubt on your part, and it is free from negative thoughts about how others perceive you. Being positive, direct, and exact in the initial approach creates a desire by prospects to get to know you personally.

It is easy to overlook the significance of perfecting an introduction and doing the little things that excite others to meet you. The priority is to overcome the receptive hurdles often prevalent in an initial introduction. Being approachable is the key. Trying too hard to make a big first impression by exerting too much effort to impress others, rather than not enough, can turn them off. Just be your best self…that will be good enough.

APPROACHABILITY INVENTORY

Here are some reminders about good "approachability" during the embryonic stage of meeting someone:

Prepare your appearance. Do you look and dress like someone ready, willing, and able to make a good first impression? In the business world, your clothes should be one notch above the usual dress of your clientele.

Prime facial expressions. Display a cheerful face, regardless of your mood. Putting a smile on your face before you leave home in the morning completes your look.

Create a "safe" environment. Enjoy being with each person. Make them feel like you would rather be with them than anywhere else.

Make eye contact. Look others in the eye--and provide a firm handshake. Shake the entire hand, not just the fingers.

Be considerate of time. Show every person you have a conversation with that you have their best interest at heart by maximizing the time you spend together. Be cautious of rushing to ask for a "yes." Ensure you have the buyer ready to be asked.

Be thoughtful of opinions and considerate of feelings. Listen to others with an open mind. You might be surprised at what you learn about others when you ask…and listen.

Call people by their names…and often. Is there anything sweeter to the ear than being called by your name? Call the person's name every chance possible. (If an older person, ask permission to contact them by their first name).

Speak and act enthusiastically. Use the three "E's" —— energy, excitement, and enthusiasm—when in a relational situation. It shows how important they are to you. And your message will carry a lot more weight.

Create early involvement for your probable buyer(s). The information provided is only as good as the info wanted— and needed—to be heard. So, discover what others are interested in by discovering what they are interested in doing. Sounds like an essential question-and-answer period?

Be patient and courteous—don't rush. Ask questions and listen. No hurry. The information learned might surprise you. It very well could save time later.

Astuteness in this area of approachability is what leads to a superb first impression. Approachability has applications across many fields of endeavor. It offers a formula for facilitating success at almost anything you do that involves building quality relationships. Make approachability a top priority. This is a rewarding first step in creating a lasting, positive impression.

An age-old axiom states: *"You can never have it any different from the way you have it until you are willing to do something you have never done before!"* Don't let the imaginary boundary within you create hesitation in expanding your horizons and taking on activities that enhance your approachability.

COMPONENTS OF A GREAT FIRST IMPRESSION:

- The right *appearance* leads to a positive *CONTACT*.
- The right *approach* leads to a positive *PRESENCE*.
- The right *attitude* leads to a positive *IMPACT*.

RULE OF THREE THIRTEEN

The Rule of Three Thirteen is one of the key steps to making a great first impression. During the introductory phase, maximize your approachability by utilizing these three rules:

- Thirteen *feet* as you approach someone accentuates the 7/11 initial impression.
- Thirteen *inches* accent the handshake, eye contact, manner, and bearing.
- Thirteen *words* accent what is said, how it sounds, what the guest says, and how well you listen.

EMPATHY

Empathy is doing all you can to make the world around you, a better place in which to live.

Making an impressive first impression is a great start. At the heart of the next step in your efforts to sustain a new relationship is employing empathy.

Webster defines empathy as *"The capacity for experiencing as one's own, the feelings of another."* Empathy is crucial...

- To be able to see things from others' perspectives.
- To create an environment where others open up to you.
- To communicate your understanding of those emotions.

Experts in the psychological field have identified three types of empathy: Cognitive, Emotional, and Compassionate. All these forms of empathy are evident in different ways and are essential to understand when developing relations with probable customers.

COGNITIVE EMPATHY

Cognitive empathy is most often concerned with the elements of thought, understanding, and intellect. It is constructive in negotiations, motivating others to act, and understanding the diverse viewpoints encountered in dealing with many potential customers.

Cognitive empathy is responding to a customer with empathy and understanding on a non-emotional level. It is defined by a deeper understanding of the intellectual level of the customer you are currently working with.

This type of empathy can be a tremendous asset when the goal is to gain in-depth knowledge of potential customers. It aids in learning what it takes to direct that person toward a specific action...the kind most needed in sales.

To truly understand another person's feelings, you must *feel* them yourself. Those who react with Cognitive Empathy risk being too business-like, but this type of empathy has its place and purpose in the business world.

EMOTIONAL EMPATHY

As the title shows, the concern is with emotions and feeling sensations. The most effective way to utilize this type of empathy is in close-knit relationships, coaching, and management situations. Exercise care because Emotional Empathy can be overwhelming for some and inappropriate for others in certain circumstances.

Emotional Empathy involves directly feeling another person's emotions. You may not fully take on another person's emotional and mental state, but the type of response offered is more intimately related to that person. This helps form a stronger bond with an individual.

For Emotional Empathy to work, you must manage your emotions. The secret is not to get too wrapped up in the feelings of others. Your role is to understand the emotional state of another, not exhaust yourself in their emotions. Emotional balance is crucial in preventing emotions from becoming overwhelming and counterproductive in your interactions with others.

You build Emotional Empathy when you possess an "I care" attitude. This engaging, accepting, and encouraging attitude will work wonders in customer and client circles. Emotional empathy should be a priority as you build a stable of connections.

COMPASSIONATE EMPATHY

This is empathy in action. Compassionate Empathy doesn't mean you completely understand a person's problem or challenge. Neither does it emphasize feeling the emotions associated with it. It compels acting spontaneously when necessary. Sensing the need and filling is its hallmark.

Compassionate Empathy is difficult to attain. It is a type of empathy that involves intellect, emotions, and action. Cognitive Empathy may be the most effective way to react in a work situation; Emotional Empathy may be the most suitable response for loved ones or in intimate relationships, but Compassionate Empathy strikes a powerful balance. This type of empathy displays the natural connection between the brain and emotions. Considering both the felt senses and the intellectual situation of a probable customer is the core of this type of empathy.

Compassionate Empathy is taking the middle ground by using logistics and emotional intelligence to respond correctly to a situation. It is wise to approach this without becoming too emotionally invested or attempting to fix things alone.

EMPATHY "DO'S"

Try these thoughts about empathy on for size:

- Applying empathy enables others to express their needs, wants, and interests freely. The more they talk, the better your understanding of them will be.

- Empathy requires patience and focused listening. Listening attentively shows readiness to understand the other person's viewpoint. Gain as much additional information as possible. Listen thoughtfully to what the speaker said.

- Empathy involves recognizing the type of feelings you have in a similar situation. Remembering how you felt in a similar situation can give you a better sense of how others might think in a similar situation. This understanding enables an empathetic approach to assisting others in similar situations.

- Empathy matures through the observation of individual differences. Be aware that people are human beings with all the personal differences that those two words imply. They have things—work, families, hobbies, and lifestyles—that they want to talk about. Allow them time to share with you all about themselves.

- Don't confuse empathy with sympathy. There is a world of difference between the two. Empathy is an attempt to understand another person, to act with reasoning and logic. Sympathy is characterized by being involved in another person's affairs—a tendency to be too involved.

Empathy is a natural part of skill development. The key trait of empathetic people is the ability to shift their focus from themselves and move it to others. They turn the switch on to be mindful of the message presented. They pay close attention to verbal and nonverbal cues that are a part of any communication with people.

How is your empathy? Empathy is one of the most excellent tools in your sales skill's toolbox. Ensure you express empathy with everyone you meet.

EGO DRIVE

A saying goes like this: *"We need more, we go and less ego."* Would it surprise you to discover that the best way to have more "we" moments is to have a strong "ego drive"? It isn't easy to function in a competitive environment without the strength derived from it.

First, it is wise to understand that ego drive differs from ego-driven. The latter person looks out for their self-interest regardless. People with a strong ego drive have a purpose—a 'why'—outside themselves that drives them to act.

In our estimation, ego drive refers to a special need to achieve. It's a means of gaining satisfaction that comes from wanting and needing to do a good job personally, apart from any monetary gain.

Those with great empathy and a strong drive for success position themselves to succeed in almost any sales and marketing situation. To possess both is not a contradiction. Quite the contrary. They make a great team.

Those with good empathy but insufficient ego drive tend to experience ineffectiveness when dealing with more demanding customers. When the *heat is on*, these entrepreneurial salespeople are likelier to use sympathy than empathy. Since they do not thrive on *standing their ground,* they find a more leisurely route and give in. Instead of a practical compromise, they feel sorry for someone and sympathize with their plight. Empathy rather than sympathy is the cornerstone of excellent selling.

Empathy and ego drive reinforce each other. With both, you have the backbone needed for maximum motivation. You want to do your best to satisfy the customer. But your goal should be to do this without empathy spilling over into sympathy. Sympathy in sales leads to giving in too early and too much.

EGO STRENGTH

Ego strength is crucial for recovering from a challenging situation that did not turn out as expected. This is especially true in marketing and sales, where the nature of the business involves not making a sale. It is often necessary to follow up after a long-standing client ends unexpectedly, opting to buy elsewhere.

A weak ego can have a detrimental impact on both current and future outcomes. Ego strength is a trigger—a motivation to keep going when the inner spirit would instead turn tail and run. Minus the bounce-back ability provided by ego strength, most people find themselves on an emotional rollercoaster.

To recap, those with little ego strength may feel torn between the competing demands of others. Those with excessive ego strength can become too unyielding and rigid with others. Striking a balance is the key. If you possess empathy, a strong ego drive, and worthy ego strength, you should do well interacting and selling to various prospective customers.

RAPPORT

Many entrepreneurs who are unfamiliar with the concept of rapport practice it daily. Rapport comes from the French word meaning *favorable contact*. Its active use in sales and marketing makes it a bonding process.

The concept of rapport implies the necessity of *"disengaging the tension"* between two people. It serves to connect two people, and that process starts with listening. The things that help establish rapport with others resemble empathy. Here's our take on establishing rapport:

- Be genuine. Be yourself. Don't try to be someone you are not. Relax. Smile. Be Positive.

- Rapport building begins with your first contact with a person. It continues with the first words out of your mouth. Make the greeting warm and friendly.

- Let us reiterate: Give a firm handshake and maintain eye contact. Be engaged, but don't force it. Be as natural as possible. Let your true authenticity show.

- Limit your talking, especially about yourself. The focus is on what others have to say. You show genuine interest when prospects do most of the talking early. Also, you gain the knowledge needed to assist them better.

- Potential customers want to share their thoughts, including their wants, desires, fears, and even their problems. They want to feel like they are being heard. You cannot talk and listen at the same time. Listen attentively to discern the message being offered.

- Find common ground. Prospects prefer to talk with those with similar interests. Uncovering similarities makes it easier to build rapport. Listen carefully to pick up similarities that will help you determine what will create a solid connection.

- Provide details. If what you offer involves highly technical information or the subject is unfamiliar, provide more detailed information to help the buyer better understand. The buyer will appreciate it, and the clarity may assist you.

- Don't interrupt the prospect. Hear the prospect out. Listen for subtleties. Give the prospect every chance to express their desires. Don't be too overly sensitive to time. Let the prospect get their point across. Once they are finished, pause a moment before speaking.

- Adjust and adapt your approach if needed. Depending on the buyer's background, adjust and adapt to build rapport.

- Overcome the natural tendency to jump from one question to another to speed up the process. Cultivate the ability to stay focused on the point under discussion until you receive a response. Practice strategic waiting.

- Pause before replying. This conveys the appearance of considering the customer's thoughts and perspective. A good practice is to restate what you heard. Focus on the salient points. It means saying, *"I really want to understand you?"* or *"Is this what you're feeling?"*

ROLE OF HUMOR

The one thing we can count on about humor is it can be a plus in social development. Because it is widely and universally accepted, humor significantly influences the development of people skills. *"Humor can serve as a 'social radar' by attracting and connecting with like-minded people."*

The Latin root for the word humor is *umor*. Umor means "to be fluid, like water." In the same way that water sustains life, humor nourishes life. It helps us to survive and thrive in times of chaos and uncertainty.

There is no question humor is a common form of human communication. The beauty of humor is that no words are needed. Show a room full of people who all speak different languages, a silent video full of humorous acts, and what is the result? How about a room full of hearty laughter!

Laughter is the universal language. It sits at the heart of humor. Consider this: there are thousands of languages spoken worldwide, but there is only one universally recognized one: the language of laughter. It is guaranteed to be understood.

Laughter is the physical expression of finding something funny in a particular action or statement. As Josh Billings once said, *"Laughter is the sensation of feeling good all over, and it principally shows in one spot."*

The impact of humor on social skills becomes even clearer with increased use. Humor is much more than creating a good laugh. Allowing ourselves to see the lighter side of life has many psychological benefits. Humor offers these benefits:

- Validates experiences, making the invisible visible.
- Illuminates how we process the world.
- Helps us to think more flexibly and reframe situations.
- Diffuses the tension around controversial topics.
- Serves as a "social lubricant" by firming social bonds.
- Engages in thinking, feeling, and speaking about the way we live in the world together.
- Helps us cope with tough situations and stressful events.
- Lightens the atmosphere where tension is evident.
- Can cushion the emotional blow of a trying experience.

Here's how I (Jim) used humor to list a home in 1993. The seller was highly unrealistic about the worth of his home; I knew better. I was not about to take an overpriced listing. I wrote the list price as he stated, then when I got to the part of the Listing Agreement where I would write in the expiration date of the contract (usually six months out), I wrote the month and day down and then filled in the year, 1998.

The Seller said, *"That's five years from now."* I then said, *"You gave me a 1998 price. I want to be around when it sells."* Believe it or not, the Seller laughed and gave me a more realistic price. I listed the home, and it soon sold. Sometimes, humor can work. If it had not worked, I could have sat back and watched another agent struggle with a grossly overpriced home.

Chapter Five

EXPLORATORY INTERVIEW

First, let us emphasize that identifying the gateway challenge is the primary factor in the exploratory or investigative interview. The solution and how you deliver it emanate from the answers you receive in your information-gathering efforts.

What is the customer's *Gateway Challenge*? Customers spend their money when they face an issue affecting their finances, time, energy, peace of mind, or quality of life. The Gateway Challenge centers around either a pleasure challenge or a pain challenge. Potential buyers seek a product that will satisfy either.

Some refer to this as a *"Gateway Problem"* instead of a challenge. Since the primary reason for buying does not always center around pain or displeasure, we prefer *Gateway Challenge. Whether* pain or pleasure, decision-making is a challenge.

Semantics aside, the key here is to discover the most urgent, high-priority challenge you can solve for your would-be customer. Finding the gateway challenge begins your efforts to help potential customers find solutions. They are painfully aware of their challenge and are willing to invest good money to overcome it.

As you will see in the next chapter, you develop your product presentation around the information you obtain from the prospective buyer during this interview.

DEMOGRAPHICS AND PYSCHOGRAPHICS

These are the basis for the type of information you desire to receive in the exploratory interview. Let's take a closer look.

Demographics is derived from the Greek words (demos) "people" and (graphy) "picture." It is used in various contexts and encompasses a range of personal characteristics and information. Demographic factors include work, income, education, home location, marital status, and family.

Psychographics is the thoughts, emotions, and beliefs that affect customer behavior. It includes attitudes, interests, personality, values, opinions, and lifestyles. Psychographics aims to understand potential customers' preferences and predict buying behavior patterns.

Your understanding of these two characteristics sets the stage for your product presentation. The ability to harvest this information is dependent on an effective questioning technique.

THE USE OF QUESTIONS

We will briefly discuss the questions needed to discover demographic and psychographic information. But first, we want to take a broad view of why asking questions is crucial to the overall sales process.

A common occurrence, particularly when attempting to elicit action from someone, is to discuss topics you believe they want to hear. Unfortunately, if you failed to get the action you wanted, it was because it did not mesh with their needs, wants, or motives. Wouldn't it make more sense to distinguish needs, wants, and/or motives before discussing the action you want them to take?

Experience has shown that most people do a poor to adequate job investigating needs and wants that fit potential customers. A critical area to get the desired results is asking appropriate questions to determine someone's motivation to act.

You must produce a solid questioning technique to develop a proper relationship with a prospect and effectively gather information. The core to asking questions that lead to achieving desired results is to lay out a plan. Whatever you do, take the time to design and practice asking questions that may save you time—and heartache—later.

The interview should NOT be off-the-cuff, so to speak. Know with certainty which questions are the most important to ask to determine whether you are talking with a potential customer.

So, asking questions is the best way to get to know people better. Questions open the gate to understanding. Your capacity to get to know others better is only as great as your capacity to ask questions and listen to answers. Think about these things:

- When you ask questions, you show a sincere interest in learning about others. It also helps them to understand better the reasoning behind their buying motives..

- Questions put you in a better position to find a proper position for developing the communication process. You don't have to guess what to talk about.

- Questions function as a way to understand perspective. Questions are windows to the minds of others. They lead to greater understanding. They inspire much greater participation in the communication process.

- Treat all questions asked of you as compliments...for if they are important enough for someone to ask—they should be important enough for you to provide sufficient and informative answers.

- We are great believers in preparing the prospect for questions before you begin asking them. Your comments should go something like this: *"Mr./Ms._____, I would like to ask you a few questions to help me better understand how I might best assist you in making a wise buying decision. Okay?"*

- Most customers don't mind what you ask them so long as it is done with few words.

TYPES OF QUESTIONS

You should ask two types of **questions**: open-ended and closed-ended. Let's examine each in more detail:.

Closed-end questions are typically objective and seek specific or factual information. They are used primarily to discover demographics.

Open-ended questions help ascertain psychographic factors. They also help draw out and explore possibilities with potential buyers. Both types of questions are needed to conduct a comprehensive interview.

Closed-ended questions will look at the essential factors in a person's life. They generally can be answered "Yes" or "No" or simply by stating a known fact. The use of the closed-end questioning technique should involve these decisions:

- What information is needed.
- What questions to ask.
- How to phrase the questions.
- When to ask the questions.

Examples of closed-ended questions are: *"What is your name? Where do you work? How long have you been there? What do you enjoy most about your work?*

By contrast, open-ended questions require thought and introspection. These are the questions best suited for finding psychographic facts. They start with the following seven words:

- **Who** creates uniqueness.
- **What** spurs narratives.
- **When** sparks a time period.
- **Which** generates a choice.
- **Where** indicates a place.
- **Why** establishes motives and details.
- **How** creates explanations.

QUESTIONS NOT TO ASK

Refrain from asking questions that:

- Presses prospects to make decisions they may not have adequately considered.

- Puts prospects in the position of defending their positions.

- Forces prospects to bail out later on in the interview to save face.

- Motivates prospects to talk about "money" before you are ready.

- Pushes prospects to answer personal questions that focus on making a decision they may not be prepared to answer right now.

BOOMERASKING: A NO-NO

Be careful of being guilty of 'boomerasking.' Boomerasking, you might ask? It is a derivative of boomerang. Boomerasking is a relatively new term that describes someone asking another individual a question to set the conversation up so the individual asking can brag about something they have done.

Here's the picture: You are conversing with someone who might become a prospect. You ask a seemingly innocent question, "Did you watch the big game this weekend?" Since the question came out of the blue, the individual may offer a casual answer like, "I watched some of it." Whatever the response, you skim over it because you want to steer the conversation in a direction that will allow you to brag about the fact you were at the game. "I thoroughly enjoyed being there. What an atmosphere!" Now, who was this about? You.

We have all probably done some "boomerasking." It is never about the other person, it's about each of us. It's about as self-centered and self-serving as any factor in a conversation can be. It is a habit that kills a sincere discussion every time. This type of manipulation has no place in a business setting.

Asking questions, listening to answers, and following up on those answers are the most powerful pathways to connecting with a potential customer. Nowhere does boomerasking fit into this equation. This form of "one-upping" is the death knell of what you hope to accomplish with a customer.

To avoid this conversational booby trap, remember the purpose of engaging in a dialogue with a prospect is not about you. It is about them and their perspective. The practice of boomerasking will ruin the magic of shared understanding and interpersonal connection you have with a potential buyer.

Often boomerasking is done with good intentions, but setting up a conversation to brag about what you have done will backfire. It does nothing to help others feel more involved in the conversation. Suspend with *'asking with the intent of bragging."*

LISTENING: THE SELLING SKILL

Are you aware that it is easier *not* to listen than to listen? Research shows that the average human can hear 400 to 600 words a minute and speak 125 to 150 words a minute.

Even with this wide discrepancy between the ability to hear and the ability to speak, we probably understand only about 25% of what is being said. This occurs because we can listen faster than the speaker can talk. As a result, we tend to mentally stray and start thinking about what to say in return.

LISTENING LEADS TO ACTION

Do you realize that you listen to people into buying, not talk them into it? Building sales and marketing skills starts with your ears, not your mouth. As you improve the quality of your listening, you enhance the impact you have on potential customers.

The quality of listening plays a vital role in building a toolbox of sales skills in the following manner:

- You learn nothing about prospects by telling, but there is no limit to what you know by asking and listening.

- The easiest route to impacting prospective buyers is not the information you provide them, but the information they give you. You see a lot by listening.

- Through listening, you demonstrate a greater interest in others, which in turn encourages them to show a greater interest in you.

- When you listen and observe, you gather more information that leads to a better understanding.

- Listening helps you pick up clues to assist potential buyers in making sound and reasonable decisions.

- Listening reflectively helps you to help others answer questions that might be on their minds.

Our Maker gave us two ears and one mouth for a reason!

LISTENING ATTITUDES

- **Limit your talking**. You can't talk and listen at the same time. Listen with your *"whole being"* and *"feel"* the spoken words. This is crucial to the overall conversation with someone.

- **Listen for thought patterns - not just words.** It's essential to listen to the point of view being expressed, rather than reacting to how it's presented. The words are important, but the *thoughts* behind them are even more important in the grand scheme of things.

- **Focus on what is being said.** As previously noted, listening speed is generally faster than speaking speed. Focus on the whole message, not the "bits and pieces."

- **Don't interrupt**. Hear the person out. Give them a "full hearing" to express thoughts and feelings. When the prospect finishes talking, pause for a moment before you speak, in case they want to add something.

- **Be slow to jump to conclusions**. Be patient. Listen to everything with an open mind. Jumping to conclusions is not an approach you should take when speaking with a potential customer.

- **Listen between the lines for emotions**. Eighty percent of what is being said is emotions. If you only listen for facts, you only receive 20% of the entire message. Listen to feelings, as well as facts.

- **Provide details**. Avoid being too technical; if your message is unfamiliar to your prospect, provide more details to help them understand better. Ask specific questions to discern their comprehension level. Then, listen reflectively so you can reply appropriately.

- **Use silence.** Silence is an excellent tool for controlling the flow of conversation. Quality listening involves pausing and experiencing a moment of silence before responding to your prospective buyer's words. (We will have more on silence later on)

- **Restate what you think you heard**. Restate the prospect's opinions or perspectives. "*Is this what you mean?*" Ask for clarification. Don't assume. If the potential buyer makes a point that is unclear to you, say: "*What I understand you are saying is this, is that right?*"

- **Ask for feedback**. Show your desire to understand the probable buyer's message by asking for feedback or clarification: "*You feel that you want _____, is that right?*" Or "*Do I hear you saying _____?*"

An exploration interview can occur whenever you feel it is appropriate to expand the relationship with a potential buyer. The primary objective of this fact-finding interview is to utilize open-ended questions to gather pertinent information that will inform and direct your sales efforts thoroughly. After a thorough investigative interview, you should have a good sense of the Gateway Challenge for prospects and a basic understanding of their needs and wants.

OTHER COMMUNICATION SKILLS

We turn our attention to other communication skills that are critical to sales success. While these are not widely heralded as essential tools in the information gathering phase, in our opinion, they are and should be on your improvement list. These are the tone of voice, word choice, semantics, and image-producing language. Here's a look.

TONE OF VOICE

Do you realize that every time you speak, you speak twice? We don't mean that you talk with a "forked tongue." We are saying that the words that come out of your mouth convey your thoughts, while your tone of voice reflects your attitude. What you say is essential, but how you say it is just as important.

Think from your own experience. You sense when someone is telling you something, but their tone of voice isn't backing up what they are saying. How often have you been on the other side of the equation where your tone of voice didn't quite match the words you were speaking?

Research has shown that as much as ninety percent of friction in our lives is caused by tone of voice. Most of the time, in our conversations with others, the tone is often separated from the impact of the words spoken.

The sales process is compromised unless the tone of voice and spoken words are in accord. The tone of voice confirms that the words spoken say what they were meant to say.

were expected to say.

Understand that the tone of voice is as effective as words in conveying your message. When the tone of voice is not in line with the words spoken, there is little to gain and much to lose.

Keep reminding yourself that words serve little genuine purpose unless backed up by tone of voice. When these two are in accord, the ability to communicate is greatly enhanced, and your message carries more weight.

Primarily, the tone of voice is an expression of attitude. Disinterest, indifference, disagreement, resentment, and the like are chiefly the reasons for a negative tone of voice. These feelings may have a right to exist. However, they do little to enhance the message you are trying to convey when the tone grinds with bitterness or even shows signs of attempted politeness. Observe the nature of the conversation and assess how you are coming across.

When you are constantly aware of the importance of voice tone in the communication process, you can begin to be consciously aware of your tone and deliberately adopt a more agreeable tone. You can more effectively seek information or make your point when your tone and words are in accord.

Just think of the persuasive tone used to make up after an argument or when you want to obtain something from a difficult person. What did you do? Didn't you carefully consider ensuring that the tone of voice matched your words? It's simple to incorporate these into your conversations.

It's not always what you say that moves others action…
It is often the way it is said that makes a difference.

SALES SEMANTICS (WORDS)

Semantics identifies the meanings of words and helps select the appropriate content. We cannot discount the power of words in our daily interactions with others. Words considerably raise the power grid in sales and command a more significant influence.

Realize that entrepreneurial sales success is measured by a *"transference of feeling."* The more the buyer feels optimistic about the offer, the greater the sales success.

More often than not, words create feelings in people. These feelings can be either positive, negative, or neutral. You must attempt to choose the correct words to maintain a positive feeling in the buyer. If the words evoke a negative feeling, then you must change course and use words that evoke positive feelings.

The search for better words is an ongoing objective. We're not recommending fancy words, just better words. Here are examples of using better words in the sales process.

INEFFECTUAL WORDS...........................EFFECTUAL WORDS

contract	agreement
sign	okay/approve
credit application	customer statement
financing	easy finance
payments	investments
list or retail price	market price
buy	own
discount	savings
problem	opportunity
termination	maturity date
deal	proposal

These are examples of words that can positively influence and evoke positive feelings in prospective buyers. A successful sale does not result until you create positive feelings for the buyer. This leads them to act because they sense they will be better off for making the purchase.

Most people have a vocabulary of about 300 to 500 words. Some have 3000 words. Nevertheless, the average daily usage is approximately 50 words. It's all about the quality of use rather than the quantity. With the prevalence of social media and electronic devices, we are witnessing a growing awareness gap regarding the importance of word selection. Consequently, it has a negative influence on the marketplace.

Here's a good dose of wisdom and a tad of wit:

- If we talk too fast, we often say something we haven't thought of... yet.

- Slow down and speak with tact, then you will have less to retract.

- We don't have to explain something that we didn't say, do we? Among our most prized possessions are some words we have never spoken.

- There is absolutely no physical or scientific evidence that the tongue is attached to the brain. That makes a wise decision one where the brain is turned on before putting the tongue in gear.

- One of the best ways to save face is to be careful how we use the lower part of it. Others don't mind what we have to say, so long as we say it in a few words.

USE UPBEAT LANGUAGE

Every congruency of words spoken creates these three thoughts in a listener's mind:

- **An attitude**
- **An emotion**
- **A mental picture**

It is wise to use image-producing words or upbeat language to convey a point of view to a prospect. This language creates vivid, alive mental pictures that can stir emotions and develop positive attitudes. Words like success, prosperity, future, win, profit, happiness, joy, and affluence lead to positive emotions. The more you use positive, imaging-producing words, the simpler it becomes to use them.

Here are points to remember that help to keep in mind the importance of upbeat words:

- You will be known by the positive words you use.

- Make sure words are understood. Explain technical terms that are outside the listener's regular vocabulary.

- Nonverbal qualities should support upbeat words.

- For words to be truly effective, body language should align with the tone and temperament of the words spoken.

- Uplifting words demonstrate conviction in the value of what you are doing, the necessity for communicating that value, and getting people to respond to it. With this kind of belief and conviction, others will listen and respond favorably to your words.

- Using positive, uplifting words gives you a better feel and perspective of how much impact you can have on your prospects' actions. Closer observation shows just how well you are doing in stirring others to action.

- Upbeat, positive words trigger positive emotions in the listener's mind. This provides a better chance for the listener to associate what is said with good feelings.

- Using positive self-talk affirms and supports your best self. Self-talk is something naturally done during all waking hours.

- Research has shown that self-talk influences emotions, perspective, and the actions taken. You are more likely to build confidence, feel more in control of events, and achieve more goals when you use positive self-talk.

"Use upbeat language often and see the difference."

INFLUENCE OF FAMILIARITY

It is only natural to be wary of something new or strange. This is especially true in human-to-human interactions. Now toss in any attempt to move someone to act, and you can see how the words chosen are paramount in ensuring those words are received positively and with feeling.

The more upbeat and uplifting words used in seeking approval of something, the more you work with, rather than against, human nature. All other things being equal, the more positive words spoken about an item, the more attractive it becomes to others.

Here's an ad that demonstrates the use of positive words: *"Discover a world of **timeless beauty** and **exquisite** craftsmanship with our **stunning collection** of **handcrafted** jewelry...Every piece of jewelry tells a **unique story**, and we are **dedicated** to helping you express your style through our **meticulously** designed pieces."*

The more often people hear something, the more comfortable they are. Familiarity works; it has been heard many times before.

Ad agencies have understood this principle for eons. They repeat the same message for an extended period because they know it works.

Your probable customers are more likely to favor familiar things over unfamiliar things. By becoming more familiar with who you are and what you offer, they will naturally become more likely to favor you over numerous other alternatives. Maximize the use of the influence of familiarity.

Keep improving your performance "groove."
Your ability to learn, grow and improve is not
marked by years – a state of mind marks it. Years
of experience will weather your hide, but to quit
learning will weather your soul. Knowledge
and skills know no age—they never grow old.

Chapter Six

LOCATING AND GATHERING LEADS

As an entrepreneur, you do not go to work,
your work is wherever there are people.

You need people. People need you. People are opportunities. People are the bridge to your future. People are your lifeline. People are the faces of your customers and clients. However, they may not realize they need you until you meet them and discuss what you offer. That is the reason the statement above is so true. Your work is truly anywhere there are people.

As an entrepreneur, the fantastic products you have available, the super program you offer, or the marvelous anything you sell are great sales beginnings. But what is your chance of succeeding without a continuous flow of leads? Your success begins and ends with the leads you gather, the prospects you establish, and the sales you eventually make.

Lead generation begins with establishing relationships with various potential buyers. From that beginning, you will work your way toward identifying the "right kind" of prospects to engage in a tactical outreach program and create interest in your products, programs, and/or services. This is at the heart and soul of your prospecting activities as you generate leads.

You can be the most knowledgeable and informative entrepreneur in your area of expertise, but nothing can happen until people are interested in listening to what you say. That makes your number one job, seeking those probable customers who can buy what you sell.

A lead generation program designed to locate new customers may be referred to as a "*numbers game.*" You need exposure to many people to get the program started. Yet, capturing quality leads is more than that. Once you get the numbers right, it becomes much more of a "*connection game.*" If done correctly, your lead generation program will focus on identifying individuals who match your ideal customer profile. The more you do it, the better you will become at it.

The secret to prospecting success is making quality connections rather than attempting to develop a large number of connections. Consider connecting with individuals who can purchase what you are selling.

> When asking an individual to grant you an interview -- regardless of the venue you are in -- always give the individual a choice between "Yes" or "Yes," never "Yes" or "No." In other words, "Can we get together this morning or would this afternoon be better for you?" Either way, you have a "Yes."

10 ATTITUDES FOR LEAD GENERATION SUCCESS

Your attitude toward prospecting sets at the core in creating the right climate for locating potential buyers. These will help:

- Lead generation involves locating and gathering potential buyers, is a way of life in sales. Welcome it because there is a direct correlation between leads generated and personal sales growth. Success in one begets success in the other.

- Accept the fact that a continuous plan to develop and improve your prospecting skills is the only way to stand out from the crowd and do something special. Making something superb happen requires quality lead generation time and effort.

- You take pride in what you do, and it shows. Excitement about what you do is a guiding light for others to be excited about, and it will ignite their desire to buy from you.

- Hold yourself to high standards and work meticulously on constantly upgrading your lead generation skills. Realize it is no soft touch—it takes intelligent planning and hard work to interact well with diverse buyers.

- Be eager to learn how to locate new prospects, then practice what you have learned. Knowledge, coupled with proper application, makes prospecting a groove—the more you do it, the better you get.

- Having a planned lead generation program serves an instrumental purpose. Because locating and gathering prospects is an inexact science, especially at the outset, discouragement and discontent can arise. Mentally stay focused on your lead generation goals, and you will soon successfully overcome negative emotions.

- The emergence of a higher level of lead generation success requires patience—a large following (or clientele) cannot be built overnight. However, a solid stable of prospects can be gathered with a persistent and diligent effort.

- Decline tactfully but firmly request to engage in time-wasting activities. Establish consistently regular times to contact people and stick to it. Be dedicated to a daily schedule for lead generation.

- Be tough with yourself. Refrain from letting the "no's" deter action toward your daily prospecting goals. Despite the "nos" you receive, continue to build connectivity and develop relationships. It gets easier the more you do it.

- Dwell on successes. This will continually encourage you to grow your prospect list.

COMMANDMENTS FOR LEAD GENERATION SUCCESS

Your role as an entrepreneur begins with interacting daily with potential new customers. These commandments are designed to provide direction as you develop a quality lead-generation program. Walk through them slowly and digest them thoroughly.

Commandment #1: Define Your Target Market. Before launching your lead generation program, it is essential to define your target market clearly. This helps you focus on what you are looking for in probable contacts and the needs they might have. It also positions you as an expert in a specific field or market.

Commandment #2: Create an Ideal Client Profile. Aim for quality over quantity in developing potential customers. Instead of concentrating on a varied list of people, focus on those most likely to become a better fit for your products/services.

Commandment #3: Be Organized. Have a personal system for organizing your lead generation efforts...and follow it. Have a computer program that helps you keep track of personal contacts, and carry a Day-Timer-type device to record pertinent information about people you meet. Always record any new contact's name, phone number, and e-mail address.

Commandment #4: Develop a power "list" of leads. These are the businesses and people you buy from, as well as individuals at church and school, acquaintances you meet through civic organizations and after-work activities, and so on. Record this list of people in a computer file. Those on this list can develop into quality contacts and lead to personal interviews. Work this list thoroughly...adjusting as necessary—dropping and adding names as circumstances dictate.

Commandment #5: Utilize a Proven Prospecting Software Program. A software prospecting program will help you automate and streamline online tasks related to generating and qualifying leads. Email finders, business-to-business (B2B) lead databases, email verification services, and live chat software programs are available to support your lead generation efforts. Establish a ZOOM account to converse with potential clients. Also, have a calendarly-type of account where you can set up appointments with prospects. Leveraging these tools facilitates the process of contacting and qualifying leads as prospects.

Commandment #6: Attend Online Networking Events. Live online networking events are among the most effective ways to establish meaningful connections with potential clients. Many of the networking events we attend are invitations we receive from other hosts. Before the event, it is wise to prepare a two-minute script of what you would like to say. Most networking events offer breakout rooms where you can exchange information with five or six people at a time. Most attendees will put their contact information in the chat. Harvest this information.

Commandment #7: Host a Webinar. Webinars are an excellent way to generate leads, qualify them as prospects, and establish yourself as a thought leader in the marketing field. Offer a free live webinar on a marketing topic that interests your ideal customer and is relevant to your product or service. The webinar is an excellent way to capture email addresses that can lead to future contacts. As the host of the webinar, you can also offer an upsell of your entire marketing program during the event, which could generate high-quality leads.

Commandment #8: Schedule a Fact-Finding Call. Make the telephone your ally. Spend some uninterrupted time daily calling potential customers. Repeat the task of calling during a continuous block of time. This helps you get into a groove. A fact-finding call is an excellent method for qualifying prospects. It typically lasts 20-30 minutes. Write a script to use for your fact-finding call. This way, you can ask prospects similar questions to determine if they are worthy prospects for your product or service.

Commandment #9: **Follow Up Consistently.** After a fact-finding call or personal meeting, follow up consistently with prospects. While some may purchase your product directly after your first or second contact, many will need more nurturing to become clients. Most often, a product demonstration is an effective way to continue engaging with a qualified prospect, ultimately leading to a purchase.

Commandment #10: Ask for Referrals. Once a prospect is converted into a paying customer, their delight with your product will be at its highest peak. There is no better time to ask your happy customers for referrals. *"Thank you for the opportunity to serve you. I would be grateful if you could provide me with the names of those you think would share your enthusiasm for your new purchase.* Do this before you leave their presence. If it is an online purchase, call to thank your new customer, and don't be remiss in asking for referrals.

THREE RULES FOR APPOINTMENTS

- **Show Up Early.** Approximately fifteen minutes is the right amount of time to arrive before a scheduled meeting or interview. This allows you time to make a restroom stop and gather your thoughts. No one is interested in your excuse for running late. Always allow for flexibility in case of possible traffic delays, adverse weather conditions, or difficulty finding a parking spot. When the time for the appointment arrives, you are ready. First and foremost, be responsible and respectful of others' time. It tells a real story about you.

- **Dress to Impress.** It has been said that a picture is worth a thousand words. Whether we like it or not, we are judged by our appearance. Ensure you portray the image that highlights your best attributes to help create the right first impression. Your clothes should be clean, fit properly, and conservative. Also, remember that proper hygiene is essential. Finally, ensure you are comfortable with what you are wearing, whether you are sitting or standing. When you look the part, you are more likely to play the part.

- **Be Aware of Your Manner and Bearing**. The non-verbal factors of posture and how you carry yourself are critical when meeting someone for the first time. Paying attention to your body movements and overall body language is essential. Your posture, a firm handshake, eye contact, and facial expressions are all parts of how you carry yourself. Your body language should be secure and comfortable.

  We recommend that you videotape yourself to watch how you walk around a room and how others might view you. You should also consider videotaping a mock interview with someone you trust. Observing yourself in this way will help you identify areas for improvement in your body language. Looking people in the eye conveys confidence and interest in what they have to say, while a warm smile is likely to be reciprocated.

OTHER PROSPECTING REMINDERS

Asking for a General Referral: *"Sam, who do you know at work that might have an interest in the product you purchased?"* Or *"Martha, you are around a lot of people every day. Who have you come into contact with lately who might be interested in (your product)?"* Or *"Dale, who do you know in your golfing group who might be interested in hearing the story about the (product/service) you recently purchased?"*

Ask about Other Family Members: *"I deeply appreciate your purchasing this (_____)from me. I would like to have the same opportunity for other members of your family.*

For my own knowledge, who in your family might you recommend I speak to? I would be very appreciative if you could provide their contact information to me.

Tell Everyone You Meet Face-to-Face What You Do: *"Hi, my name is _____ ___. I'm in the business of marketing a very unique (product). Here's my card. On the back of the card is a note about something special I will do if we can get together for a visit, or if you recommend someone else to see me.* (Pause to provide the person a chance to respond) *Thank you for your time. I look forward to seeing you very shortly."*

Take the 'Curse Off' a Telephone Call.:. *"Mr. Customer, this is Mary Salesperson. Did I catch you at a good time?"* Or *"Ms. Customer, this is Joe Salesperson. Did I interrupt something important?"* Then, continue with the purpose of your call.

"I'm very Busy...I don't have Time to Talk Right Now." *"I can appreciate the fact that you are busy, but what I want to share with you might (what's your hook?). Would this afternoon or tomorrow morning be a more appropriate time to call?"*

Provide the Prospect an Option: *"Would it be more convenient to meet in the morning or in the afternoon?"* Or, *"Would you prefer to come in this afternoon or would tomorrow afternoon be better?"* (NOTE: *Always provide the prospect with a time option;* you stand a better chance of obtaining an appointment).

TELEPHONE DÉCOR

Some rules that it would be wise to follow. Never call before 9:00 am, between 11:30 and 1:30 pm, between 4:30 and 6:30 pm, and never after 8:30 at night. Why? These are times people set aside to be with friends and family for meals, and the time they get up in the morning or prepare for bed in the evening.

Simply put, these times interrupt people from doing what they almost always do EVERY DAY! It is also a wise decision never to call whenever a "big game" is being televised.

INTERNET PRESENCE

Do you have a viable *"Internet Presence"* and online sales strategy? Hopefully, yes. As a reminder, you need to be where the competition is. The web is no different. You cannot do business today without an internet strategy and knowledge of exploiting its potential. But the key is knowing how to manage the present and future simultaneously.

An "Internet Presence" is more than having a website. It comes down to how you handle the leads, the quotes, and the requests made by internet users. You gain attention, instill confidence with a great website, and raise the users' expectations. You must be prepared to *"work the internet"* if you take advantage of the opportunities presented by the web.

After all, it is simply an online showroom, and that's all you want it to be. You want buyers to know about your inventory and how to contact you via email or phone to make online purchases, if your product or program presents that opportunity. If there is no online service available, ensure that you provide an alternative. Otherwise, it will be more difficult to find quality prospects.

There are numerous top tools to supercharge your internet prospecting efforts. These online prospecting tools can be used to track, qualify, and converse with prospects. The best tools typically are B2B lead databases or email lists that offer verification and lead scoring. Check them out.

Many CRM (customer relations management) platforms and sales pipeline software also offer prospecting features. Ask around what's available and what others are using. The internet provides numerous options to explore.

ARTIFICIAL INTELLIGENCE

In today's world, artificial intelligence is more than a buzzword; it's a tool that dramatically enhances an entrepreneur's business. Opinions vary widely about the role of AI in marketing and sales, with some even questioning if AI will replace the need for much that an entrepreneur does. That doesn't seem to be the case in the opinion of most experts. AI will be a great assistant.

Therefore, our take is that artificial intelligence capabilities will not replace salespeople. However, it will be a vital part of selling in the future, notably in lead generation.

Since AI has a future in sales, wise entrepreneurs will incorporate the AI process into their daily activities. Those who fear ending their careers due to AI's inclusion are more apt to lose out to those who maximize their sales efforts by using AI. The sooner you get started, the better.

The pairing of Artificial Intelligence with a real-life entrepreneur who has learned when and how to harness AI's enormous capabilities is a winning combination. AI-powered marketing will benefit entrepreneurs who sense the favorable predictability of using AI in all aspects of the sales process.

Is now the time to leverage AI's capabilities for yourself? There is no question that the ability to keep up with and challenge the competition will require the use of Artificial Intelligence. This will definitively be evident in the field of prospecting. It is for real. Those entrepreneurs who embrace AI in prospecting enhance their capabilities in identifying the right people to sell to.

AI will analyze and process data on potential prospects at incredible speeds. Based on data analysis, it can also customize prospect information and tailor communication to individual prospect needs and wants. The key factor appears to be that AI's output depends on the quality and accuracy of the data input.

ADVANTAGES OF AI

- **Automation.** AI can handle routine tasks such as scheduling and data entry. This frees entrepreneurs to focus on more in-depth and complex tasks.

- **Data Analysis.** AI can quickly and accurately analyze vast amounts of data. When AI is employed to analyze data that aids entrepreneurs, sales strategies and better decisions will result.

- **Customer Personalization.** AI can personalize customer data, making it easier to prepare for an interview.

- **Uncover your ideal customer profile.** AI insights help you accomplish this. Use it.

- **Design the perfect hook.** This one would captivate and compel quality action.

- **Create a table of contents and a narrative flow.** Ensure it resonates with your customers.

- **Optimize** each item to capture and maintain reader interest. You can also organize and refine anecdotes and stories to add life to your presentation content.

HOW TO USE AI

If you write emails, letters, or postcards, you can use AI to refine and/or correct your writing. You can even change what you have written to another person's format. For example, to see how this can be applied in your daily business, write a letter to a person in your database or to yourself. Save the file. Using your browser, search the internet for ChatGBT.

You can use this service for free, but your time and document length will be limited. Keep your message concise and clear. Then, in the text box on the site, enter 'Convert Text to Dr. Seuss' after you have uploaded the letter file you saved earlier. You will be amazed at what ChatGBT (AI) will do to your message.

It's fun to experiment with other famous entities, such as Einstein or Donald Duck, or to enter the Convert test in a more professional language. Play with it to test and see what works. You might find it to be a worthy tool.

It is essential to establish distinct points of difference between your organization and its competitors. In this regard, it is highly recommended that you take courses available in most communities on AI, business accounting, income taxes, etc. You must be learning-based to stay ahead; otherwise, your competition will pass you by and leave you in the rearview mirror.

KNOW YOUR NUMBERS

How many customers or clients do you need to reach your sales goals? AI can undoubtedly automate the labor-intensive activities required first to discover the desired number and then understand the necessary number to elevate your sales. This is a method for estimating the number of calls and contacts you will need to make to improve your sales numbers.

For example, how many people do you need to present to before you can sell what you are selling? How much time does it take to secure that one buyer? How much does acquiring that one buyer cost you in terms of time and money?

If you know how much money you want to earn for a year, knowing these numbers will tell you exactly how to go about achieving it. It will also inform you of the number of people you must contact and make a presentation to, to close the sales needed to reach your annual income goals.

When you know and understand your numbers, you can calculate precisely how many people you will need to maintain in your database. Then, this position determines how often people in your database must be contacted to find the number required to make a sale. This is not guesswork; it is an exact science, and AI can undoubtedly help you maintain accurate numbers.

The use of AI can significantly enhance your marketing efforts. Explore various AI programs that align perfectly with your lead generation plans. It makes it easier to locate prospects and more productive when you do. Utilize AI if you haven't already done so.

OTHER NUMBERS THAT COUNT

How many people would attend your wedding if you were getting married today? This question is odd but crucial to understanding the "numbers game." Most people typically have between 250 and 300 guests at a wedding.

These figures represent your initial database of people you know, which will become your database of potential buyers and/or sellers. Of the 250-300 people present, approximately 25 could be considered your inner circle.

If they needed what you are selling, these people would never go anywhere else but to you to make a purchase. These people could be considered as your primary wealth builders. Regardless of your sales approach, once you identify the inner circle of people, you must keep them informed about everything you do. More importantly, approach them one-on-one.

Explain to your inner circle people that your big-picture goal is to build a successful entrepreneurial business. Tell them that it will be impossible to reach your desired goals without their help and input. By help, we mean to ask them to be on the lookout for anyone looking to buy what you sell. Instruct the inner circle on how to initiate the initial referral process with their contacts and then advise you of their names so that you can follow up with them. Share your inner circle of successes, including the training you are engaged in, conferences you have attended, and awards you have won. Keep them posted on your career path. Make them feel a part of your success.

DEVELOP "CLIENT REFERRAL PROVIDERS"

Those in your inner circle can help to jumpstart your lead generation program. However, once you have built a customer database, you have a new source of information available to assist you in prospecting. Your ability to convert customers into clients will help you develop and create your own "*client referral providers.*" These "*client referral providers*" are individuals who have purchased from you and with whom you have established solid relationships.

As the quality of your after-sales follow-up with customers increases, their confidence in you also increases. With this growth in confidence, those customers move toward becoming clients. Clients differ from customers in that they enjoy a different kind of relationship, which can lead to a client becoming a "*client referral provider*" for you.

As a "*client referral provider,*" your client becomes your enthusiastic, loyal supporter. Your client actively endorses you, your product lineup, and your service. But most importantly, that client refers others to you on a regular and continual basis.

Whether you recognize it or not, when your customers buy from you, they also buy you. You "*made*" your customers want to do business with you. You earned their trust and gained their respect. They believed in you as an entrepreneur and a human being. You do such a good job of selling yourself that most of your customers would feel ashamed to even think about doing business with anyone else!

Why shouldn't you take advantage of your customers" tremendous belief in you? Wouldn't they want their friends to do business with you? They know you will treat their referrals professionally. All you have to do is ASK your customers to provide you with a referral (s).

The chances of your customers having a name on the tip of their tongues will be rare indeed. You must "coach" them by asking about specific functions your customers engage in, such as work, play, church, or civic club activities.

Statistics show that the referred prospect is the "*easiest to sell.*" Be active in this area. Select a handful of your good customers and ask them something like the following:

1. *"Sam, who do you know at work who might be interested in the same buying opportunity you took advantage of?"* Be firm when requesting a referral.

2. Martha, you come into contact with *many people every day. Who have you come into contact with lately who has been talking about buying (what you sell)?*

There are many other possibilities you can use. Think up your own and give them a try. The important thing is to do it -- and do it regularly. There are *"client referral providers"* just waiting to assist you with your lead generation program.

"CATCH PHRASE"

Do you have a *"catch phrase"* about your business that is easy to use and remember? I (Jim) use the phrase, *"Thinking Real Estate? Think Gymbeaux.com."*

That phrase serves several purposes. First, it associates me (Gymbeaux) with Real Estate (my business). Second, by simply creating an internet URL address out of my name, prospects now associate my company (real estate) with my real estate name (Gymbeaux) and my internet address (Gymbeaux.com).

Typically, the new contact will ask, *"Really, tell me more!"* That opens the door rather than closing in on what you do and their fear of someone attempting to sell something they have no intention of buying, YET!

WORDS MEAN THINGS

We have used the terms *"potential customers and potential buyers"* throughout the book. Jim ran across a word that author and trainer Jeffrey Gitomer suggested that people in sales should consider using. Instead of referring to leads as *"potential,"* begin the mental training process of referring to them as *"probable."* When you start to think of people as *"probable buyers,"* you have already begun mentally preparing them to buy from you. This is undoubtedly something to consider using.

QUESTIONS TO ASK REFERRED PROSPECTS

Getting the conversation off to a good start with a referred prospect is crucial. Here are a couple of suggestions for introducing yourself to an individual who a client of has referred:

- *"Mr./Ms. Prospect, my name is Jane Entrepreneur. I'm associated with (company name (if you are the Owner or President, say so). (Name of client who made the referral) gave me your name and suggested I give you a call and introduce myself. Did I catch you at a good time? Or do you have a moment for me to tell you why (name of client) suggested I give you a call?"* Pause for response, then react accordingly. Given a *"green light,"* continue:

We shared with you earlier the importance of asking open-ended questions. These questions help you better uncover your prospect's needs and wants. They also afford the chance to ask follow-up questions that uncover additional important information.

Prep the prospect before asking questions: *"Mr./Ms. _____, I would like us to walk through a few questions together. That way, I can better understand how I might best assist you in making a wise buying decision. Okay?"*

Devise an open-ended question for your prospect for each...

Why:_____

Who:_____

What:_____

When:_____

Where:_____

Which:_____

How:_____

AN UNBALANCED PROCESS

Locating and gathering prospects is a very unbalanced process. There is no balance -- regardless of the product or service—between contacts and people who are in the market to buy right now. You will not connect with a ready-to-act-now prospect, for example, on every fifth call.

Sometimes, you must ride out 15 to 20 "Nos" or "Maybes" in a row before finding one quality prospect ready to do business. Yet, the others are still prospects for "down-the-road" activity.

The secret to prospecting success is in the times you succeed...not the times you fail. You may not see the results of your hard work right away. Stay the course, and your success will increase dramatically over time, providing ample opportunities to make sales.

NETWORKING

One of the major focuses of in your role as an entrepreneur is detailing how to establish and build workable relationships through networking. *"A network is key to your net worth."*

Networking can powerfully impact your ability to attract people with similar interests. It can make a difference in attracting, sustaining, and maintaining relationships with people who are a good fit in your professional and personal life.

You are responsible for pursuing client/customer goals with dedication and determination. However, often factors beyond your control necessitate a different path.

Building a quality network is an art, not a science. Give it your very best effort, but do not become fixated on a preconceived notion of what to expect. Your efforts could lead to an unexpected outcome, It might even be better than what you originally thought.

Networking success requires strengthening your openness, awareness, respect, and the importance of connectedness to others.

Creative involvement with others is the key to discovering and unleashing relational potential. It is also a route for gaining a greater sense of self-identification. Growth in one leads to growth in the other.

The secret to developing a network of eminence is your ability to attract high-quality connections rather than numerous connections. Professionally, connect with those individuals who can play a vital role in your network.

WHAT NETWORKING DOES...

- It provides an opportunity to help others.

- It enhances your knowledge base.

- It opens the doors to new outside opportunities.

- It helps to become more visible to the right people.

- It puts you in a position to get more quality feedback.

- It is a place for support when needed.

- It paves the way for professional success.

- It elevates your reputation and builds trust and support.

BUILD A REFERRAL NETWORK

A referral network is crucial for identifying new customers. Used properly, your networking leads can have a powerful impact on your ability to attract the kind of prospects who fit your client profile. The following will help in your efforts to develop a referral network that can keep you busy:

- **Integrate Networking into Your Daily Activities.** Growing a referral network is more than a byproduct of developing a quantitative list—doing it daily is essential and effective. Don't let your referral network develop as just a by-product of doing business—work on it daily.

- **Organize Your Current Network.** If this is your first venture into networking, your beginner's tools include a mail list, internet social networks, e-mail lists, phone indexes, address books, business cards you have collected, and correspondence files. Take the time to identify those on any list you might have who you think would be a good fit to contact regarding your product or program.

- **Encourage Involvement By Those Close To You.** Be actively involved in networking with the people closest to you. Promote your business to your family, closest friends, and former business associates.

KEYS TO NETWORKING

The following should help your efforts to develop a referral network to increase your contacts and connectivity with clients.

- **"Ask and You Shall Receive."** Finding willing networking partners begins with asking all those in your *"sphere of influence"* to assist you...whether they are potential customers or not. The Law of Asking says: The more times you ask, the more 'Nos' you will receive, but your 'Yeses' will also dramatically increase.

- **Raise Your Visibility.** The key step in building a network is increasing your exposure outside your *"sphere of influence."* Put yourself out into the community. Be serious about building a network. Let people know who you are and what you do.

- **Approach People Enthusiastically**. Others are more apt to engage in activities that will benefit you when you are enthusiastic. It will open many doors.

- **Interact with Strangers.** Approach people with vigor and enthusiasm. Focus on learning as much as possible about a new contact. Ask questions and listen. Do you share experiences and interests? What might you help them with? (See the last point).

- **Provide Your Elevator Talk.** Once you decide to talk to the right kind of possible customer for your product or service, then you can provide information about what you offer.

- **Stay In Touch.** Getting folks to join your referral network is one thing. Keeping them providing you with referrals is another. You must stay in touch regularly.

- **Seek referral partners.** Getting individuals to join your referral network is one thing. Keeping them providing you with quality referrals is another. Inspiring and frequent contact will help keep them actively engaged.

- **Take the time to express your gratitude.** Continually say "Thank you" to those who assist you. This will strengthen the bond and encourage continued strong efforts from those members of your network who offer referrals.

- **Be strong and flexible.** Always remember why you are seeking new customers. Entrepreneurial achievements are built on the determination to move forward and improve as you progress continually.

- **Offer your help.** Ask a prospect who sells a product this: *"What can I say to my customers that might be interesting to them about your business, your service or your product?"* It may shock the prospect.

YOUR APPROACH

Your approach to new probable contacts is key. Our number one rule as you approach potential new buyers is not to talk about your product or service first, but to get the potential customers to talk about themselves and their business first.

Here's a greater opener: *"I'm really impressed by what you and your company have accomplished. Tell me, what has helped you get to this point?"* People love talking about themselves, their businesses…and their successes. Take the time to engage the potential prospect in the conversation and listen to what they have to say. Use reflective listening to let others know you are listening.

Then, you can follow up with a *Gateway Challenge* question (more later): *"Mr./Ms. Prospect, what do you see as your biggest challenge going forward?"* Your interest lies in the challenges you can help solve and how you can assist a potential customer in achieving even better results.

Words alone cannot convince prospective customers to trust you. Trust is something you must earn. Asking, rather than telling, opens the door to developing a profound understanding. Trust is enhanced when you know customers personally. This position allows you to discuss what you are selling in greater detail.

Trust empowers you to meld yourself with future customers. It helps establish a platform for a deeper understanding of prospective customers, making communication with potential customers more comprehensive and practical. There is a built-in connection that goes beyond dollars and cents. That connection embraces trust. It is the secret to togetherness.

You want the world of people who need you to be involved with a confident and socially competent you. Your ability to reach out toward those possibilities depends on developing the skills required to maximize your networking opportunities. Your total approach is to facilitate doing the things that will lead to maximizing your efforts.

Effectiveness in developing, building, growing, and sustaining a quality network is the centerpiece of entrepreneurial growth. Significantly expanding your network and progressing over time is key to building a substantial and diverse network of solid connections and relationships.

ABC OF NETWORKING

The ABC of networking is **A.lways B.e C.onnecting**. Making a connection starts what you want to accomplish going forward. Job number one is to create connections with the *"right kind"* of people. The environment which you meet someone says a a lot about that determination. Make networking a daily practice. "It is both a 'connection' game, and a 'numbers' game as we have mentioned several times. Be ever vigilant in your pursuit of potential buyers.

One way to accomplish this is to use another "point of difference" tactic discussed in the PROLOGUE. Offer something FREE to anyone visiting your website or reading your marketing and/or promotional material. Lou offers a FREE Ebook entitled THE LAUGH, GIGGLE, GRIN, AND THINK BOOK (A tad of wit and a whole lot of wisdom). It has over 1,250 one-liners covering all aspects of life. There is a landing page where people can download the E-book simply by registering their email addresses. What can you offer?

You do this by offering them an article on something that is eye-catching or may be tied to their business. The beauty of this is that you provide something of interest, free of charge, simply by people sending you their name, email address, or text message to your email address or phone number. Be creative in what you offer, and hopefully, it will set you apart as a "point of difference."

A FINAL THOUGHT

"How will I know when I come in contact with someone who might be interested in your business, your service, or your product?" How many salespeople have you ever met who asked you that question? They want to assist you! Try it yourself. Offer to help your customers who sell something to the buying public. That may lead to some surprising consequences.

Chapter Seven

CLIENT-FOCUSED PRESENTATION

Most entrepreneurs new to sales excel in this area. They feel at home and present what they offer with enthusiasm and excitement. The information here will help you refine your sales presentation to make it more effective and profitable.

A good way to position yourself to deliver a quality, client-focused product presentation is to understand why customers buy and how they make purchasing decisions. Learning both is crucial to a higher level of success. This knowledge organizes your ability to ask skillful questions and listen carefully, identifying the dynamics behind buying decisions.

Once you understand the "why," you can effectively structure your product/program presentation to address the "How" that leads to a purchase.

People buy for their own reasons. Every buying action a person takes is aimed at improving their relative condition. Each buying decision is an attempt by that person to be better off for having made that decision. Psychologically, no person can want to end up worse off than before.

WHY PEOPLE BUY

Here are some things you should know about why prospects make the buying decisions that they do:

- You grasp that people buy things for their own reasons...but depend on you to help them clarify them.

- You decide how to tailor your overall product/ program presentation to each buyer.

- You gather the information that leads to creating a presentation that adds greater interest to each customer.

- You gain a deeper understanding of potential objections a prospect may raise.

- You come across as a salesperson with high knowledge and believability.

- You get more meaningful sales results with a more effective presentation.

THE BUYING MOTIVE LEVELS

Mental level: economy

The customer who buys at the mental level is interested in:

- Reduced expenses...

- Lower costs...

- Increased efficiency.

Physical level: safety/security

The customer who buys at the physical level is interested in:

- Freedom from harm...

- Reduction of physical risk...

- Being secure.

Emotional level: social/belonging

The customer who buys at the emotional level is interested in:

- Being in style...

- Feeling important...

- Winning the approval of others.

Psychological level: esteem/self-actualization

The buyer who buys at the psychological level is attracted to:

- Well-engineered features...

- Top-of-the-line/hi-tech options...
- Reputation of the product.

We mentioned earlier that everything we do as human beings arises out of a need to either avoid pain and/or lose something on one side or enjoy pleasure and/or experience gain on the other. Most of us are torn between these separate forces when making important decisions. We want to gain, but don't want to risk losing.

Your position in marketing is to establish sound, quality reasons why and how you can help each prospect gain and improve. No one consciously makes a buying decision to be worse off than they were before. Prospects want you to do this without making them feel like you've "*sold*" them; instead, they want to feel like they've "*bought*" from you. There is a difference.

THE FIVE P'S OF BUYING

To buy anything, a person must move through the five (5) P's or mini-buying decisions before buying. The decisions are:

- **PURPOSE:** What is the purchaser's purpose (need or want)? Needs/wants are the basic factors that put a person in the market. Needs and wants are based on a desire to enjoy certain benefits that a person is currently not experiencing.

- **PRODUCT/PROGRAM:** What product will fit and fill the need? This decision is based on advertising, word of mouth, finances (ability to buy), and a salesperson.

- **PLACE/PERSON (SOURCE):** Whom should the customer buy from? This question has a three-tier answer: You, someone else, or no one. Mostly, the source is a salesperson who: 1) knows their business, 2) provides a quality product presentation, and 3) offers a price that is in step with the acquiring business.

- **PRICE:** Price is closely related to need and product. Only after a customer's mind is clear on these two issues can they relate the quality and value of the product to the price tag.

- **PERIOD OF TIME:** Is TODAY the right time to buy? Without an agreement that *"now is the time to buy,"* something is amiss with one or more of the other buying decisions. If NOW is not the time to buy, your task becomes one of isolating the primary reason to *"why it is not the time to buy."* The decision could be delayed forever until you ask for the prospect to buy and determine the purchase status.

Why is it important to know the five buying decisions?

- No purchase is made until the prospective customer has said "yes" to each of the five buying decisions.

- Your knowledge of the five buying decisions will chart you through every product presentation and the handling of each prospect's buying motives.

- It shows what remains to be done to obtain the prospect's okay. Every objection offered will refer to one of these five buying decisions. If it doesn't, it is not an objection.

- When you identify a decision a buyer is struggling with, focus your efforts on it until you feel comfortable you have addressed it properly.

KEYS TO A QUALITY PRESENTATION

- The key to a quality sales and marketing presentation is to sell the buyer, not the product or the price. If your presentation is product or price-focused, where you continually discuss the product's merits and/or the price, selling can be challenging. If your sales presentation is customer-focused, selling becomes much easier because you tailor your presentation to the customer's basic needs, wants, and buying motives.

- When your presentation is customer-focused, you help the prospect make the connection between the value, quality, and price of the product. You establish a solid connection between the product features and the benefits that meet the prospective client's buying motives. This point is crucial to the sale's success.

- A quality presentation depends on it being a two-way experience. Get the prospect (or prospects) involved in the selling process. Learn how to share your product so that ideas and information are moving in both directions between you and potential customers:

  "Do you see how that works?" Do you understand how that would benefit you and your family?" These are examples of how to get the potential client involved in the purchasing process. And it helps you gauge their buying temperature.

USING PRODUCT KNOWLEDGE WISELY

Using product knowledge wisely begins with recognizing that the key to sales and marketing lies in focusing on the customer, not the product. In other words, buying decisions become more challenging if your presentation is product-focused and you continue to present feature after feature to the prospect. However, if your product presentation focuses on the features that interest the buyer, decisions become more manageable.

By tailoring your presentation to the customer's needs and wants, you help the customer better connect the value and quality of your product and/or services to the price paid. You establish solid connections between features and the customer benefits.

You rarely create interest through product knowledge alone. The essence of being knowledgeable lies in how you apply your knowledge. What you know is only good to the extent that it helps you obtain a new customer. It is not what you know about your product that counts… it's how you use it when it counts.

PRESENTATION ESSENTIAL

- First and foremost, always be enthusiastic. Enthusiasm is a personal quality, but it is never purely individual. It affects not only your performance but also positively affects your prospective buyers. Remember: When you divide your enthusiasm, it multiplies.

- **Present a cheerful face.** Enthusiasm radiates a vibrant glow. Give your smile a chance to work. The only place a poker face is an asset is in a poker game.

- **Say what you should say…not what you could say.** Limit your words. Let your product do the talking. Buyers prefer the specific to the general, the definite to the vague, and the concrete to the abstract.

- **Speak convincingly.** Put excitement in your voice…raise and lower your tone. Deliver your words powerfully.

- **Vary your speech pattern.** You typically increase your speaking rate when you are excited and enthusiastic. Speaking more slowly on key points will emotionally draw the listener closer to you.

- **Be animated.** Don't be afraid to use gestures and express your enthusiasm for your product or program through body language. Displaying how you feel enlivens your product presentation and is better received by the prospective customer.

- **Listen reflectively.** Provide feedback as the prospect talks through both verbal ("Yes, I see") and nonverbal (nod of head) methods. This will get you involved and keep you involved in the process.

- **Say what you mean quickly.** Enthusiastic entrepreneurs hit the main points and move on. Highlight how your product/service will benefit the customer now and in the future. Also, express yourself with depth and conviction. A wise move is to talk little and say much.

- **Be sincere.** When sincerity is absent, enthusiasm lacks a solid foundation or genuine meaning. It becomes a facade that others can see through easily. Believe in what you're doing, and your excitement and energy will shine through every time.

A good sales presentation is more than a simple pitch. It's a differentiating tool for moving prospects toward a buying decision. Discover how to effectively leverage the power of your sales presentation to influence decision-making and drive sales growth.

PROPOSAL ALIGNMENT

Your ability to present your product or service in a logical sequence facilitates understanding, builds value, and cultivates desire. We call this a *Proposal Alignment*. This is how you align your presentation within the context of the prospect's specific buying motives and the gateway problem/challenge.

The information you obtained from the *Exploratory Interview* outlines how to arrange your presentation so that it makes sense to your potential customers. Your proposal alignment should be asked with these questions in mind:

1. What is it that you propose?
2. How does your proposal address the *Gateway Challenge*?
3. Accent the benefit of each proposed feature to a customer?

The *proposal alignment* should be tailored to each customer. This helps the sales figures to fall into place because your proposal is aligned with the potential customer's challenges. The alignment of your offer should reflect the primary challenge or craving of your ideal prospects. You deliver the solution for the outcome they want…and need.

THE S.E.L.L. TECHNIQUE

The use of a proposal alignment plays a crucial role in creating a high-quality sales presentation. Your proposal alignment provides a clear track to follow as you present the virtues and value of your product and/or service. I (Lou) labeled my sales presentation, the S.E.L.L. TECHNIQUE. It still has merit.

This technique is a proven method for product presentation. It offers a proposal alignment that will make sense to both the customer and you. When you have an established sales platform, the actual execution of your presentation becomes more manageable and better understood by the probable customer.

S.tate the Feature/Option. A feature or option is a part of the product/program, and explaining it in greater detail is essential. This is based on the answers you receive when you are using a questioning technique. For example, if safety is a crucial buying motive, the prospect is likely to be drawn to the apparent safety features.

E.xplain the Operation of the Feature. How does the feature operate? Demonstrate or explain to the prospect the functions of the feature or option and how it operates. Ensure you understand the concept before proceeding to the next feature or option.

L.ift Desire with the Benefits to the Client of the Feature. Please don't leave it up to the prospective customer to guess how a feature or option will benefit them. Explain the benefit using one of the four Buying Motive Levels. This is a crucial factor in your proposal alignment.

L.eave with a Positive Question. *"Do you see how this will benefit you and your family?"* or *"That's definitely* *something you want to have, isn't it?"* These questions will build a series of "yeses" in the prospect's mind, making it harder for them to say "No" when you ask them to buy.

S.E.L.L. KEYS

- When discussing a product feature, look at the feature. When sharing how the buyer will benefit from the feature, look at the buyer.

- As a reminder, tell a prospective client what you can do—never what you cannot—unless asked.

- Once you have identified the most appropriate buying motive, build and reinforce the features that best fit that buying motive.

- Devote a lot of your selling time to the few features that fit the buyer's perceived buying motives. This means you will commit most of your time to the features that will bring a buyer closer to saying "Yes."

- Focus on one feature of the product at a time, explaining the operation/advantage and the benefits of that one feature before moving on to the next.

- When selling to a male and a female, accent the proper operation of a feature primarily toward the male and stress the benefits to the female.

- Do not assume a prospect knows how a particular feature operates. Explain the linkage between the feature and the operation/ advantage.

- Be confident that the prospect understands the feature and its benefits before moving to another. Never assume.

- Somewhere in your presentation, talk about the product as if the buyer already owns it. For example, "**Your** _____ has these outstanding features." Get into the habit of using "You" and "Yours" to build mental ownership.

BE FLUENT IN SILENCE

Silence is a super marketing tool. When you ask a prospect to buy, and the prospect is slow to give you an "okay, what is your best tactic? When you are worried because the prospect doesn't appear to be responding like you want (or as quickly as you would like), the best thing to do is--nothing! Keep calm!! Don't say anything! Show some patience. Let SILENCE work for you.

You will *wait* your way into a lot more orders than you will ever talk your way into. So don't forget, once you have asked a buying question, keep silent and give the prospect time to respond. Silence is a great friend in creating a new customer.

You shouldn't be afraid of momentary silences anywhere in your presentation. If you read that a prospect is thinking about some phase of your proposal, stop talking and let the prospect think. DON'T INTERRUPT! Silence, please...until the prospect is ready to continue. Then ask: *"Is something on your mind that I can help you with?"* The key here is not to be afraid of a moment of silence. It is a good way to let a prospect open up and say something to help make a sale.

The message is plain: Use silence purposefully. It's vital that the will to ask for a "Yes" is there. The ambition to ask is necessary. Summarizing key benefits counts, too. The one essential to any excellence in obtaining business repeatedly is SILENCE.

Wait for the client to mull over the offer you've given so it can sink in. Then ask again for the order and WAIT. Silence is golden in the realm of sales success. It is worth its *wait* in gold.

Prospective buyers do not want to be given the 'facts' alone...they want you to inspire them to make what they want to be attainable... appeal to their reason, but, more importantly, stir their emotions— probable buyers are moved more by the depths of their feelings than by the height of their logic.

Chapter Eight

HOW TO GET TO "YES"

Thousands of sales opportunities are lost daily for one simple reason. When right on the threshold of creating a new customer, some entrepreneurs tend to flinch...back off...retreat... and lose courage at the very moment that it is imperative to A.S.K. for a buying decision. The future of any sales opportunity is always uncertain. But by asking for a "Yes" decision, you provide yourself a more significant opportunity to add a new customer. Doesn't that help make the future less uncertain than it would be?

One of the most significant discomforts you experience in selling is feeling like you have done everything right to attract a customer. Still, it did not materialize in the way you would expect after rendering such an excellent presentation. You are probably wondering why the recipient of your wonderful message failed to respond to your proposal. The unpretentious answer is straightforward: you failed to ask the customer to make a purchase.

It is common to find salespeople who risk losing potential clients because they fail to ask the probable buyer(s) to make a purchase. The significant question here is this: Isn't it better to have the courage to ask and attempt to make something happen than to fail to ask and make nothing happen?

The measure of a sales leader is the ability to perform at a high level, regardless of the circumstances, but most notably in closing situations. Discipline yourself to concentrate on doing your best on every sale, under every circumstance. No one closing situation is ever more than another—they all are essential.

THE A.S.K. THEORY

It is essential to understand that asking potential clients to buy has been earned and is relevant when you are prepared. **A.S.K.** is an acronym. It stands for:

A.ttitude

S.kills

K.nowledge

A.ttitude. Unless you are committed wholly and entirely to the marketing concept, your proposal alignment of the products and services you offer—will fall flat, and your growth will be slow at best. The attitude toward all these areas is contagious, and when it is correct, your enthusiasm and passion for what you are doing will be a significant factor with your customers.

Skills. Even when your attitude is positive and your excitement level is high, you can still get hit with a dose of reality—namely, a whole bunch of NOS that can fracture your desire to continue asking. Find two or three skill methods for asking and practice them until they become second nature.

K.nowledge. How well do you know your products and services? Can you present them with confidence? What you know and how you convey it to customers puts the finishing touch on the **A.S.K.** Theory. Your ability to ask will grow as fast as your ability to translate your knowledge into customer action.

COURAGE TO A.S.K.

"Is the courage to ask for a "Yes," a challenge for you?" If the answer is "Yes," then take the lead of the successful entrepreneurs around you who tapped into their deepest resources to find the courage to do what they were formerly afraid to do.

The magic formula for developing a way to deal with present challenges is to have a "*now courage*" attitude. Just A.S.K. the prospect to buy. When you have provided a potential client with every reason to buy what you offer, what keeps you from taking the initiative and asking? Doing it regularly puts you into the rhythm of things. The first thing you know, asking for a "Yes" will be second nature to you.

PRINCIPLES OF ASKING

- Enter the A.S.K. phase of the sales and marketing interview with the attitude you never get anything you don't ask for.

- Since you will only have what you are willing to A.S.K. for, ASK! If you wait for the "right time" to ask the prospect to buy, you probably will never ask.

- The more committed you are to acquiring new customers, the simpler the A.S.K. becomes. Stay committed throughout, with the attitude that you will gain a new customer.

- A prospect's wallet is closer to the heart than the brain...meaning you must move the prospect in your direction *emotionally* before you can get to "Yes."

- Focus on the potential buyer's needs and challenges ...not what monetary reward you will get in return.

- If you have an internal set of expectations to obtain the prospect's approval, those expectations alone will increase the likelihood.

- If you display signs of nervousness, defensiveness, or confusion when you are ready to A.S.K. for a "Yes," the buyer may experience the same feelings.

- The closer you get to asking the prospect to act, the more critical it is to know what NOT to say and what to say. Watch your technical terms when a possible "Yes" is on the line. At this stage, always comment on what you can do, not what you cannot do.

- Customers are not something found...they are something created—one "Yes" opportunity at a time.

- Revisit the value and quality of the product/service through a microscope and the cost through a telescope.

- Keep your cool. Do not become frustrated if things are not going as well as you like.

- Respond...don't react. Gain control by asking questions. Use questions to maintain control throughout the process.

- End on friendly terms—even if the prospect fails to purchase from you. This is a good time to ask for a referral, even from a non-buyer.

- Long after your presentation has ended, prospects will not remember your words, but they will remember the way you made them feel.

THE GOLDEN RULE OF ASKING

The most crucial weapon you possess in asking the buyer for a "Yes," is knowing how to balance persistence with respectfulness. Being doggedly determined to obtain a "Yes" doesn't mean you have to suspend treating buyers as you would like to be treated.

The secret is learning to continually seek a "yes" within the rules of elegance and courtesy. If you have made an excellent presentation and your product/service fits the buyer's needs and wants, haven't you earned the right to persist in seeking a "Yes?" Keep asking professionally without being offensive. There is a difference. Learn it. Use it.

HOW TO A.S.K. APPROACHES:

DIRECT APPROACH: *"Bob, let me get some information to get us started. In what name will we be registering your new _____?"* Then ask for the potential customer to provide their *"Okay, right here."* Point toward the signature line. *"Carol, all I need is your okay right here (point toward the signature line)."* Place the signing pen on the contract or agreement right by the signature line…and then shut up!! (Never ask the customer to *"Sign here."* That term portrays too much "legalism")

SUMMARY APPROACH: *"Mark, let's review the reasons we've agreed on that support your decision to act today." (After summarizing the buying points, use the DIRECT APPROACH above to ask the customer to take action).*

LITTLE DECISION APPROACH: Ask questions about the probable buyer, confirming their interest. For example, *"Betty, how could this benefit you and your family?"* This approach is designed to get the customer to say *"Yes."* It makes saying the big "Yes" at decision time one more effortless to make. *"All I need is your okay right here."* (Again, place the signing pen to point toward the signature line).

FEAR OF LOSS APPROACH: This strategy capitalizes on the desire to avoid a loss because of a) A special program that will end soon, b) A product that is in short supply, c) Any program or product with an element of finality. Just be sure your reasoning is factual and believable; otherwise, this approach will backfire.

SET-UP FOR CUSTOMER

I, Jim, have always taught my real estate agents to set the customer up to be asked if they want to buy. If they have been prepared in advance, seeking a "Yes" becomes more natural. *"Mr. & Mrs. X, as we tour the homes on our schedule, with your permission, I will ask you if you would like to buy the home we are viewing. Is that okay?"* With an affirmative answer, as I showed the home, I would remind the potential buyer of their agreement and then ask if they would like to proceed with the purchase.

NEGOTIATING A DEAL

Some of you might have a negotiable item. If that is the case, here are some suggestions on how to negotiate more profitably:

- Never write down the prospect's first offer unless it is the full price you are asking for the product. It is viewed as a sign of acceptance on your part.

- Get the buyer to raise the first offer if that price is less than you are asking.

- If the prospect offers to split the difference. Counter back with a *"split the split."* For example, if the difference is $1,200 and the offer is $600, counter with another split of $900 at a *"split the split"* of $450.

- You can always come down to maximizing your limited authority. If you have no final decision over pricing, team up with the prospect to make an offer that the pricing decision-maker will accept.

- Turnaround is fair play. Anytime the buyer asks for a concession, you want to get something in return...that is the attitude that you need to possess.

- Make price adjustments that do not end in either 0 or 5, for example, $207. Using an "odd" number makes the prospect think you are at or near a rock-bottom price.

TRIAL CLOSE STATEMENTS

A trial close is simply that —it tests the water. The more you make, the better. A trial close will sound something like this:

- "What do you like best about the _____?"
- "How did you like the way _____?"
- "Can you see the value of _____?"
- "Is it safe to assume you like _____?"

The more trial closes you make, the more chances you have to be successful.

BODY LANGUAGE IN SELLING

"Humans do not communicate by words alone."

Add body language to the equation. Body language is an unspoken language that speaks volumes about the probable customer and you. It has much to say about feelings, as do the words and tone of voice with which they are spoken. The secret to great selling is to appreciate and understand body language.

There is a technique called *"mirroring,"* where the salesperson assumes the same posture, hand and arm movements, and head movements of the customer during a sales interview. The salesperson must be careful not to make the mirroring so obvious that the customer catches on to what's happening.

If you employ "mirroring," do it subtly. You will be able to position yourself to send a signal that the customer unconsciously picks up. This makes the exchange of information much more relaxed and acceptable.

I (Jim) have used this technique in over one hundred recruiting interviews, and I noticed that the recruit becomes far more relaxed because they feel as if they are looking into a mirror, and what they see in the mirror is what they like. This creates an environment where the person being interviewed is more open in their discussion and answers my questions more freely. It definitely has an application for sales used as well.

It is not body language, but while we are on the subject of language, it is vital that you also speak the customer's language. To avoid unnecessary communication clichés, ensure your words match those of your probable buyer. Learn to eliminate unnecessary barriers whenever and wherever possible—notably in the communication process.

The reality of spoken words is that they have no meaning except those given by the listener.

NON-VERBAL FACTORS

Often, the following nonverbal factors convey a story that is even bigger than words and tone of voice could ever tell. The reason is that they are more visible:

- **facial expressions**
- **gestures**
- **body movements**

These statistics underscore the significance of nonverbal communication. Experts in communication prepared them. These experts reported that the communication of true feelings about something is done in this fashion:

- **7%...words**
- **38%...tone of voice and voice inflection**
- **56%...nonverbal actions**

Let's review the reasons why it's vital to understand nonverbal communication:

- Determine whether what is said is being received positively or negatively.

- Learn if the other person is open or defensive, interested or bored with what is being said.

- Observe whether the other person's body language aligns with their spoken words.

- It helps prevent jumping to erroneous conclusions about what the other person is thinking.

- It can indicate a change in course or a different approach to make a point.

- The body language tell-tale signs have already told the real story if you have been looking for them.

- It simply makes selling easier.

A potential buyer's series of related body movements and expressions will provide a more accurate picture of how your presentation is being received. Pay attention, and you will reap surprisingly greater rewards.

Congruency is the key. Be attentive to a series of related movements and gestures where body language may contradict what the words are saying. Similarly, nonverbal communication is often present and tells a different story than the signs of feeling an individual display but is not yet ready to admit or discuss.

. The wise practice here is to be observant. Then, you prepare how you want to react and speak accordingly.

OTHER VITAL NONVERBAL ACTION

Action	Meaning
No eye contact	Concealing something
Raised eyebrows	Questioning what was said
Lowering eyebrows	Disapproval
Rubbing nose	Doesn't believe what is said
Stroking chin	Trying to make a decision
Pulling/tugging at ear	Indecisive
Hand over mouth while talking	Struggling with the truth
Arms crossed tightly on chest	Defensive; unwilling to act
Repeatedly wetting lips	May not be honest
Tapping or drumming fingers	Impatient; wants to move on

Chapter Nine

HANDLING RESISTANCE

What separates promising entrepreneurs from the great
ones is how they handle it when the prospect says "NO."

PSYCHOLOGY OF NO

"No!" "No!" "No!" Do you realize that by the time we reach 18 years of age, most of us have been told "no" 17 times more often than we have been told "yes"? Some of us feel that all those "Nos" have also extended into the sales portion of our entrepreneurial careers.

How are you at dealing with the "Nos" you hear? "No" comes in varied ways, but it always sounds the same. It hits us squarely between the eyes. That's because we want to be liked. We want to be accepted. We simply prefer not to hear the word "No." But "No" is part of the human condition in many areas of life, notably in entrepreneurial sales.

Success is measured by managing internal "Nos" and external "Nos. We have already determined that the major thrust of your sales role doesn't begin until potential customers say "No!" That is an external NO. Unfortunately, the most significant hurdles entrepreneurs must overcome to grow their sales results are internally generated. Those are the internal NOS.

Most entrepreneurial salespeople are incredibly unaware of their vulnerability to the fear of NO. They rarely consciously consider how this fear affects their ability to obtain new business. There is little question that the fear of NO can be a real factor in your inability to generate the kind of sales numbers you desire.

ANTICIPATION

Success in most sales situations is often measured by how effectively you manage objections when they arise. The ability to react quickly and effectively accelerates the decision-making process, providing an edge with the more difficult prospects. Anticipating what might happen improves your ability to react within a reasonable reaction time.

Reaction time is simply the brief interval between initiating an objection (the action) and determining how to react to that action. The one constant here is that a delay in anticipation, regardless of the situation, can significantly impact your response time. It is worth consideration.

What is the key to maximizing reaction time? While some salespeople may be more skilled at addressing an objection, developing anticipatory skills enhances the ability to react quickly and effectively.

Quality anticipation requires attentive presence in the present moment. A constant and deepening moment-by-moment mindfulness during the sales action will lead to more appropriate and quicker responses. The lack of complete focus and concentration adversely affects anticipation and reaction time. But when you anticipate what may happen, you maximize reaction time. The more you are attuned to the buyer, the more productive you become.

The ideal way to become more anticipatory is to possess a more present-tense mindset. You can train yourself to focus solely on the present moment. Consciously focus on maintaining your attention on the task at hand. The more you focus on the present, the more alert you become to potential outcomes, resulting in quicker reactions and responses.

Whatever you are doing, focus on what possibilities may arise. Raise your attention and energy to the highest level possible in every moment you are involved in the action. This will enhance your consciousness and elevate your level of sales activity. You will actually think of things you have not thought of before.

There is an interesting characteristic about objections. There is a limited number of them you regularly hear: *"That's too much money." "I'm not sure this product (or program) is for me." "I'm not interested in anything right now."* These are legit objections because they specifically relate to one of the buying motives.

But most statements, classified as objections, are simply put-offs, excuses, and smokescreens. They sound like this: *"I want to shop around," "I need to talk it over with my business associate,"* or *"I've got to discuss it with my spouse."* Since there are only a limited number of real objections, you can learn how to anticipate them, plan for them, and prepare an intelligent response.

Reasonable anticipation is a primary reason some entrepreneurs are more successful at managing objections than their less successful counterparts. Knowledgeable entrepreneurs have a way of anticipating objections before they arise, and they are rarely surprised by the objections prospective buyers raise.

It is not so much knowing the real objection in advance as it narrows the number to one or two. Based on your experience and/or what you have learned, listening to the buyer aids anticipation. By listening to the types of questions asked and the answers given, it becomes easier to anticipate the objections that may arise later. This allows you to nip them in the bud before they arise and create concern.

We have determined that the best way to handle objections is to address them before they become objectionable. Let's consider an example: if you are selling a large-ticket item, you first need to determine if the person you are speaking with is the decision-maker. Does this person require additional approval before making a purchase? Knowing this is crucial; otherwise, you may be speaking with the wrong person.

A fun question to ask about money is *"Will you be paying cash today?"* If it is a large ticket item that may appear to be funny, but it is a great way to (1) identify just how the customer will be paying for it and (2) if there is an approval process involved, such as the approval of someone within the company they work for or the acquisition of a real estate loan or mortgage.

> ### The height of success in managing objections is measured by how many "Nos" it takes before you call it quits.

FIVE REASONS BUYERS OBJECT

Remember the rule about objections. Unless they refer to the 5 P's of buying, they are not an objection...but a put-off or smoke screen. Those 5 P's, as mentioned earlier, are **Purpose, Product/Program, Place/Person, Price, and Period of Time.** The reasons why buyers object relate straightforwardly to the five buying decisions. The five major objection categories are:

- **No need**
- **No desire**
- **No trust**
- **No money**
- **No hurry**

Which of the following are true objections?

1. _____ *"That price is too high."* (In relation to what?)
2. _____ *"I'm not sure I like that color."*
3._____ *"Before making a decision, I need to talk to my..."*
4._____ *"Is that the best you can do?"*
5._____ *"I want to think it over."*
6._____ *"I want to shop around."*

Which ones did you select as legit resistance? Well, it is 1,2, and 4. The rest are not objections. They fall into other categories.

The best way to deal with those that are not legit objections is to ask the prospect a question. For example, *"I want to think it over."* You then respond with this: *"May I ask you what it is that you would like to think over?"* It cannot be handled as resistance until you can pinpoint what the prospect wants.

SEEK A FINAL OBJECTION

You have handled an objection a prospective buyer raises—then they bring up another one or a *"put-off"* or two. This game of "put-offs' can continue until you take action. Here's an idea for bringing this scenario to a head by seeking a final objection: *"Well in addition to that, is there any other reason that causes you to hesitate about buying today?"*

FACTS ABOUT RESISTANCE

- **Resistance is raised only when prospective clients are interested.** That's true. Why would someone bother to object unless they were interested in making a purchase or decision? So, look at resistance as a gift. Objections permit you to learn about a buyer's most profound concerns. it points you in the direction of *"What next?"*

- **Resistance is something you create.** Most likely, you haven't thought of it this way, but when the potential buyer offers resistance and raises objections, it is something you create. That is because the buyer can only resist what you say about your product/service.

- **Managing resistance—in any form—is a state of mind—an attitude.** Since it is an attitude, it can be changed and improved with practice. If you truly believe you can succeed in managing the resistance you receive along the way, then it will not weaken your approach. Realize that objections tend to strengthen your ability to stay the course and upgrade your selling skills. In time, you will be very good in handling resistance questions.

- **Never fear resistance...it helps you discover the buying temperature of a prospect.** It is not how serious a prospect's resistance is that determines your ability to cope, but how you see it and how you choose to handle it. An objection is truly a friend in disguise because it provides clues as to the buyer's thinking...and it will serve you well to look at it that way.

- **Resistance is a buyer's way of putting a momentary halt to a potentially stressful decision.** Objecting gives the prospective buyer a chance to catch their breath. Your momentarily backing off provides a little breathing room for the buyer. Give the buyer a chance to process the situation. Strategic waiting is a plus.

- **Don't fake an answer.** If you don't know the answer that satisfies the buyer's reason for resisting, say so. But tell the buyer you will get an answer ASAP, and then go to work to find the answer.

- **Use common sense.** An objection is not rejection; it is a request for additional information. Handle the objection pleasantly and intelligently—even if it sounds critical or unfair. Never argue—*"reason with, and not against a buyer."* That will serve you well every time.

- **Resistance is 80% emotional and 20% rational.** Now, where will you focus your appeal? To the emotional side, right? When you have your mind fixed on obtaining a new client, this attitude will take you right through the prospective client's emotional resistance ...and you will keep going as if everything is all right.

- **"Resistance can stop you temporarily...but only you can do it permanently."** Work hard to deny yourself "easy exits." Then "persist when they resist." The wise decision is to look at objections as guideposts—not stop signs. as steppingstones—not stumbling blocks.

- **It is always too soon to quit.** Something to remember that will help you persist when the prospect resists is this: If you treat an objection as an objection, you will have an objection. If you treat an objection as an opportunity, you can move the effort forward…and do it with gusto.

"Translate every tough objection into NEXT …for when you encounter resistance, it doesn't mean STOP… it simply means the buyer is not ready to buy—YET!"

OTHER THOUGHTS ON REJECTION

We all want to be liked and accepted. That's part of the human condition. But it is a fact that rejection is a part of an entrepreneur's life when involved in sales and marketing. Yet, feelings of rejection can be—and should be—temporary. Rejection is not so much feared as the result of rejection.

Rejection comes in many forms and ways…but it always sounds the same. The bottom line is it means *"No."* A solid way to go right through the varied forms of "No" you receive and stay the course is to take the following to heart:

"WHEN PROSPECTS SAY **NO**, THEY MAY
MEAN NO FOR **NO**W…BUT THEY
MAY LACK THE **KNO**WLEDGE
TO MAKE A DECISION **NO**W."

Be thankful for the challenges, obstacles, hurdles and difficulties you face daily. How could you rise if you had nothing to rise above? How could you overcome tough times if you had no tough times to overcome? How could you see how much you are worth to yourself if you had no obstacles to surpass? If it were not for all these roadblocks, what in the world would you do with yourself?

Chapter Ten

FOLLOW-UP

Look at the Follow-up call as the Nurturing Call...
it means the prospect needs more nurturing.

What really is follow up? Why follow up? Who follows up? Follow-up is a fascinating topic in sales, perhaps because it is what distinguishes successful entrepreneurs from the average. Studies show that almost nine out of 10 entrepreneurs fail to follow up with prospective buyers who failed to buy.

Why do most entrepreneurs fail to follow up? Fear of rejection or disappointment discourages most follow-ups. Others think that if the prospective buyer has said "No" once, why should I believe they will say "Yes" later? Here's a truism: If the follow-up time appears uncomfortable, it is probably the best time to do it

Tell prospects who fail to buy from you the first time that you will follow up. *"Please expect me to follow up with you to address any additional questions. If you prefer to call me, here's my card with my phone number."* This should enable the potential buyer to feel more confident about the follow up.

How should you follow up? In today's social media world, follow-up takes on an entirely new dimension. Texting seems to have surpassed calling or email as the best way to initiate follow-up.

Why text? The person's cell phone is rarely more than an inch away from them. An alert sound commands the eyes to read the text regardless of interest. Perhaps a response from the prospect is warranted, and they may provide valuable information to help you make a sale. You will never know unless you text.

Emails are not always read, and as the day goes by, they become buried in a barrage of other emails that are eventually deleted. Phone calls are subject to being classified as spam, robot, or potential solicitation calls. As a result, they are either blocked or deleted and rarely receive a response. However, you may want to call to confirm.

Follow up gives you a second chance. The timing may not always be right for the buyer. However, until there is a "STOP" in the text, continue with the "Follow Up."

FOLLOW UP CONTACT (Customer who did not buy)

TEXT: *What would it be if you had to pick one thing that would prevent you from returning to buy from us?" Or "What was the primary reason you didn't find our offer attractive enough to buy?*

PHONE: *"NAME , did I interrupt something important?" (or) "Did I catch you at a good time? This is (YOUR NAME). I wanted to get back to you to review what I felt you liked about our (product)."*

(Customer tells you they are no longer in the market)*:*

CUSTOMER'S NAME, if you should ever change your mind, please call me (you have my card handy). By the way, do you know anyone who might be in the market today for (our product?"

Follow up is rarely to only one person. What an interesting thought. Your follow-up with one prospect might penetrate the social lines of many people. How often do we recommend a product or service we favor, but have never used ourselves?

Knowing that following up with one prospect might reach many more people is encouraging. How positive is that for you? Your texts, Facebook, Instagram, or X accounts make this so easy.

A day of not following up with potential buyers is a prelude to lost sales. Don't waste the opportunity for a possible future sale.

KEYS TO PERSUASION

Without a lot of fanfare, these five principles serve to be of assistance in the ability to persuade the buyer who is sitting on the fence, weighing options:

- **Authority.** Most people trust salespeople who are not hesitant when presenting information. Express yourself with forthrightness and confidence. These are audible and visible signs of expertise or authority, making you more credible in the eyes of potential customers.

- **Reciprocity.** Do you have something you can offer as a free sample? Take advantage of the instinct to reciprocate–the feeling of indebtedness. Offering a token favor could lead to a bigger payoff.

- **Change.** It is human nature to cling to a presentation with which you feel comfortable. While you want to be consistent, be careful not to become monotonous. If times and conditions warrant a change in how you present your product or program, make the change. Be ready to make moderate adjustments along the way to ensure your presentation is tried and true.

- **Validation.** What proof do you have to back up your claims about the wonderful product/service you represent? Today it is easy to use the internet and a website for validation purposes…but isn't it the human touch that ultimately caters to the *"me factor?"*

- **Identify.** We are all more apt to be influenced by people we like or identify with. That is the real premise of person-to-person marketing. Many achieve tremendous success because of the connections they make.

The most challenging person to beat is the one who doesn't think about quitting and doesn't know its meaning. General George Patton once stated, *"The greatness of an individual's strength is measured by that individual's tendency to surrender."*

You can take it to the bank: *"Persistence prevails when everything else fails."* What does persistence mean to you? Our definition is the ability to keep going when you need to keep going after you think you have done all you can do. It's better to read that one again, because it's the key element of follow-up.

How persistent are you? It takes a lot of heart, nerve, and fortitude to hang in there when things go very wrong and you have very little to cling to, except a little voice telling you to "HOLD ON!" Staying the course happens when your heart is bursting to overcome and succeed at what you are doing.

Digest these crucial words: *"Nothing in the world can take the place of persistence. Talent will not; nothing is more common than unsuccessful men with talent. Genius will not: unrewarded genius is almost a proverb. Education will not: the world is full of educated derelicts. Persistence and determination alone are omnipotent,"* said President Calvin Coolidge.

We know this about you. Deep down on the inside, you have all the ingredients that it takes not to be a quitter, to not give up at the first sign of resistance, and to be willing to deny yourself easy exits because you know you have what it takes to hang tough. We know if you keep working and believing, you will emerge stronger and wiser on the other side. Persistence has an excellent track record of overcoming resistance.

Hanging tough is cut from the fabric of persistence and woven with perseverance. There are no challenges in life immune to this combination. You will go as far as these two attributes allow you to go.

"Resistance wilts under persistence."

Chapter Eleven

SERVICE IS A PRODUCT

Okay. You have received a "Yes" and now have a new customer. What will it take to turn that customer into a client? Future involvement with customers recognizes that service is a product. Effectively maintaining a relationship with customers after they have said "Yes" is essential in turning customers into clients. The service part of the equation sets the tone.

Aiming to deliver exemplary customer service is one thing, but unless your competition provides poor customer service, you need to go further to stand out truly. What is your *"point of difference?"* The wise move is to *"do all you are expected to do, then a little bit more."* With customers' expectations constantly rising, *good* is not good enough if better is possible.

What are the consequences of being inattentive to customers who have bought from you? *"Out of sight, out of mind"* is the death knell of repeat business. The following results of a survey taken several years back tell a story that is still true today about why those customers who bought from you may never buy again:

- 1% Die.
- 3% Move away.
- 5% Unable to qualify to buy again.
- 9% Product/Service dissatisfaction.
- 22% Move to another product.
- 60% indifference due to lack of follow-up.

Look at each customer as someone you can do something for, not take something from.

STAY IN TOUCH

Learn this lesson early and well: never let indifference be a reason for not securing a client. Staying in touch and following up with customers gives you several very distinct opportunities:

- The opportunity to build trust and goodwill.
- The opportunity to minimize competitive influences.
- The opportunity to ask for—and receive—referrals.
- The opportunity to correct actual/perceived problems.
- The opportunity to develop a client.

Never let indifference or lack of interest on your part be a reason for a customer/client not to buy from you again. Building a stable of quality clients develops *from* a system where you stay in touch with customers regularly and continuously. They will eventually fade away unless you maintain contact and continue to work diligently with them. They will certainly not be telling their friends and neighbors about you.

PRACTICE CUSTOMER MAINTENANCE

Taking care of customers is a maintenance practice, not a preventive practice. Dealing with troublesome areas before they arise is more effective in building efficient and effective relationships than is complaint management.

To ultimately manage the quality of service you provide to a client, you must manage each moment of *service reality*. A moment of reality is any instance where you can improve the quality of your relationship with a client, whether that assistance is face-to-face or behind the scenes.

Each moment you spend with a customer can be an opportunity to enhance your reputation with that customer or diminish it. At every moment, you must provide service. The reality of how you deliver the service is essential because it allows you to take steps to mature and grow the relationship.

Your goal in customer service is straightforward: do everything possible to deliver an outstanding service experience for every customer. The epitome of excellent service is delivering more than you promise rather than promising more.

There is nothing to compare with the moment of service reality in linking up with your business's future success. When you maximize follow-up time with a customer, you make significant strides in converting that customer into a client — and you ensure good relations and future business.

To make each moment of service count for the most, make these a part of your interaction with customers:

- Be mentally available—whenever you are with a customer…be ever-present.

- Be mindful of your customers' attitudes and feelings. Observe carefully.

- Do all that they expect of you—then some.

- Gain a broader understanding of what your customers do so you can help them grow their businesses.

- Consistently work to improve your skills and techniques in dealing with your customers.

- Remember: You do not deal with customers–you deal with an individual customer—one at a time.

- Treat every customer as if that customer were both your first – and your last.

- Be good to all your customers and you will have better customers who become quality CLIENTS.

HANDLING PERCEIVED PROBLEMS

It would be wonderful never to receive a complaint about a problem, but that doesn't fit reality. The reason *why* clients offer complaints focuses on one of the following:

- The embarrassment caused by a product defect.

- Shoddy treatment by you or someone acting on your behalf.

- A perceived promise that was not fulfilled.

- Failure to meet the customer's product/program /service expectations.

- The belief that the correction of a problem or satisfaction of a complaint will not be handled effectively.

- Failure on your part to communicate in a channel that customers can understand.

WHERE IS EACH PARTY COMING FROM?

When a customer/client complains about a "problem," whether real or perceived, or complains about the quality of care, at least these two things are on that client's mind:

- *"I don't like it!!*

- *"What are you going to do about it?"*

A significant way to answer these questions is to first "take the curse off" the situations. A statement like this will help *"_____, If I were in your situation, I would probably feel the same way."*

You, on the other hand, have this to consider in dealing with a customer's concerns:

- What is the nature of the problem?

- What mistake was made?

- What can you immediately do to help the situation?

- How can you retain the customer's business and increase productivity by resolving the issue?

- A great tactic: *" Obviously, you have a reason for feeling the way you do." Do you mind if I ask you what it is?"*

RULES TO SERVE BY:

- In serving others, let the Golden Rule…rule!!

- Customers are your most important asset, and your next customer is the next one.

- Answer the question on the tip of every customer's tongue: *"What's in it for me?"*

- Customers rarely care about how much you know until they know how much you care for them.

- Treat your customers with kindness and approach your work with professionalism.

- Don't say so much about what you want to say as what customers need to hear.

- Reminder: Always tell a customer what you can do to help — never what you cannot do.

- Communicate with customers in a language that they understand.

- Show customers how excited you are to do business with them—the best way to develop new clients.

GUIDELINES FOR HANDLING UPSET CUSTOMERS

It would be ideal if everything went smoothly with no concerns perceived by either customers or clients. But that is not reality. These guidelines are tested and proven:

- In a face-to-face meeting, talk to an upset customer privately …if at all possible.

- Get the upset customer to sit down. (Customers are less demonstrative when sitting down than when standing).

- Allow the customer ample time to air their problems and concerns.

- Keep your cool…even if the customer appears to be unreasonable and irrational.

- Express what you believe you heard the customer say… repeat back in your own words. (Then ask if that is what the customer is attempting to say).

- Attempt to ensure that both you and the customer are on the same page—both understand and are understood. Use reflective listening.

- Empathize and demonstrate a genuine desire to help solve the problem.

- Maintain your dignity in the face of an emotionally charged and irrational customer response.

- Focus on finding a solution to the problem you face. Inform the customer about the options available. Explain what you plan to do (or have done), who will be involved, and how soon you expect to have a remedy.

- Use the "buddy system" when you have reached an impasse with a customer. Is there someone else you work with who can help?

- Remember: long after the incident has ended, the customer will not recall what was said, but they will recall how you made them feel.

Chapter Twelve

FAIL FORWARD

Admirable as the idea of making a sale every time is, no one can sell them all. Losing a sale is inevitable, but what matters most is how you mentally react to the loss.

The price is high. After experiencing a loss, what you think is often the determining factor in how long it takes to disconnect from the loss and bounce back.

Before a team can learn what consistently winning is all about, it must first learn how to lose. It must learn how to quickly bounce back after a loss—notably one where everyone on the team knew they should have won.

> *"Failure can be defined as a wrong that leaves an impression that turns you in toward yourself. To come up on the losing side of a sale has no consequences going forward unless you let it deter you from moving on to the next sales challenge."*
>
> Dr. Bob Everhart

Successful entrepreneurs are not the ones who are not afraid of losing a possible sale, nor the ones who never lose one...but rather the ones who learn from their loss and move forward-- who go on despite setbacks, learning all the while the lessons that minimize the chances of losing a sale...again.

THOUGHTS ON HOW TO FAIL FORWARD

The one thing that sets entrepreneurial champions apart is their ability to use setbacks as opportunities for growth. They maintain this supportive feeling even if they give their best effort and come up short. It provides more incredible determination to right the ship and seek the next challenge. The lessons learned from occasions when you lack success can serve as a driving force, helping you refine and strengthen your efforts in the future.

Here are some "fail forward" thoughts:

- Failure is simply a mental process—a state of mind.

- Admitting that you were less than your best is a sign of strength, not a confession of weakness.

- Talking like a failure increases the chances of failure.

- Think: *"When I fail, it doesn't make it a failure. It is just a learning experience...and nothing more."*

- You will best be remembered by the times you succeed, not by the times you fail.

- When you come up short, it is crucial that you refrain from personalizing it by putting yourself down. The best policy is always *"separate you from what you do."*

- Let the past pass. A lost sale only affects the next opportunity if you hold onto that loss.

- Always "fail forward." Never look at a failure or loss in any other way than as a fulcrum for learning, so that it will enable you to learn and grow from it.

- When you fail, don't fail to learn the lesson.

> ***You can think you will make a sale, or you can think you will not. While the former does not always guarantee success, the latter pretty much guarantees failure.***

FORGETTERY

How effectively do you let go of the past and move forward? Selling is full of difficulties, setbacks, and failures. One of the things that will help you reach beyond these things is to learn how to use your *forgettery*. Your *forgettery* is a marvelous tool to put your losses and setbacks in the rearview mirror and reach out for something better.

One of the first things your *forgettery* helps you do is to let go of those less-than-successful moments experienced in the past. If you worry about the sales you fail to close, you will be closing the doors on your career before it starts. Your *forgettery* enables you to strip away the accumulative layers of "lost sales" that may have hampered you up to this point.

Of course, you still remember those bad events. There's nothing wrong with simply remembering those negatives that were part of your past, but recalling them and dwelling on them are two different things. The key is storing those memories.

When you employ your *forgettery*, you emphasize the fact that the past has passed, so it is no use continuing to dwell on it in the mind. Nothing can be done to change what has happened, but there is definitely something that can be captured from it to brighten the future.

How about you? Do you consider the fundamental and essential premise that setbacks can almost certainly offer positive benefits and lessons? Within each adverse event is the innate potential of something much better. It may be hidden, but it is there. The challenge is to unfold the great treasures of potentiality within the "negatives." Sometimes, it may be painful to look at, but do it for your future.

Once you understand how to benefit from the past, you put your forgettery to work and move on to the next level in your growth and development. With your forgettery, you discard the misstep, setback, or loss. It is a thing of the past. It's time to move forward, to expand, and to reach a new level of growth.

Okay. How do you use your *forgettery*? You must trust your own nature to untangle where you may have been all tangled up, thinking of the "negatives' in the past. You need to do two things with the past: learn from it, then run from it.

A real benefit of having a good *forgettery*, is that you conserve mental energy. Reacting emotionally, whether to a good or bad situation, eventually takes a toll on your mental approach. The result: You become increasingly more prone to mistakes, and your current actions will reflect the lack of productivity. This, in effect, will change the future outcome of your sales results.

Utilizing your *forgettery* helps to keep you on an even keel, neutralizing the tendency of emotional swings. You refrain from getting too high or too low.

That doesn't mean that you never demonstrate an emotional response. Indeed, there are specific times and places where a reaction is appropriate and necessary. Any display of emotion should be done judiciously, with emotional stability and purpose. Your *forgettery* helps.

UNTANGLE THE TANGLED

Life is full of difficulties, setbacks, and missteps. So is sales. One of the things that will help you reach elite sales status is learning how to untangle the complexities of actual negative experiences. Mentally, you must view setbacks as steppingstones rather than stumbling blocks.

One of the first things you can do to untangle the tangled is to let go of those less-than-successful moments experienced in the past. Outstanding entrepreneurs have learned how to strip away all the accumulated layers of negative things that have happened to them up to this point in time. They have learned how to use their *forgettery* to put it aside and move on.

Of course, you still remember those bad events. There's nothing wrong with simply remembering those negatives that were part of your past, but remembering them and dwelling on them are two different things. The key is learning to use your forgettery and finding a place to store those memories.

The past is behind you, so dwelling on it in your mind is useless. Although nothing can be done to change what has happened, something can be learned from it to enhance your sales future. Your weak moments are only as strong as your memory of them. Remember: *"New beginnings come from old endings."*

How about you? Do you consider the fundamental and essential premise that setbacks can almost certainly offer positive benefits and lessons? Within each adverse event is the innate potential of something that can bring improvement. It may be hidden, but it is there. The challenge is to unfold the great treasures of potentiality within the "negatives."

Once you understand how a past failure can benefit you, you can move on to the next level in your growth and development. Discard the misstep, setback, or loss. It is a thing of the past. It is time to move forward, to expand, and to strive for a new level of future growth.

Okay. How do you untangle the tangled? It's a private issue that only you can untangle, where you may have been entangled in thinking about the "negatives" of the past. You need to do two things with the past: learn from it and do your best to run from it.

> *The best thing that should come from a*
> *setback is the feeling you do not like it!*

FAIL FORWARD PROCESS

Grasp the fact that to be successful, make losing a breeding ground where you learn what it takes to turn failure into success. Since some failure in the enactment of succeeding is a given, you must make every effort to strive to fail forward.

The "fail forward" process has three very distinct stages:

1. **Awareness Stage**. *"I should not be doing... (whatever needs to be done differently)."*

2. **Acceptance Stage**. *"I should be doing... (options of what you should be doing)."*

3. **Action Stage**. *"I will... (specify what you will do to bring improvement to your performance)."*

> What matters most when an opportunity slips away is how you respond to it. The price is high because it is not the regrettable setback that carries the highest value, but your thought processes about the lost setback. The key factor is how long it takes to mentally recover and get back on the road toward preparing for the next opportunity.

A real understanding of what happened, after it happened, it provides a path to learn those things that enable you to make something more promising happen.

RECOVERY CAPACITY

Hopefully, we have distinguished that failure to do something that should or could have been done is a great learning force. That depends on being up to the task of learning from it and then applying what you learned to produce better future results.

Sales develop in an environment where you maximize the use of your forgettery and then utilize the power of your recovery capacity. Recovery capacity centers on your ability to bounce back by focusing on the "teachable moment" that losing creates. When you lose, make sure not to lose the lesson. Your recovery capacity leads to increased productivity and efficiency going forward. The sustainability of the recovery depends significantly on how resilient you are.

The key element of your recovery capacity is focusing not on what has happened but on what can happen in the future. Lessons occur more readily and quickly when your recovery capacity is open to constructive instruction. Through this openness, you can learn what it takes to make more sales, moving on to the next sales opportunity with increased vigor, vitality, zeal, and mental acumen.

"You cannot be a winner acting like a loser...and the more comfortable you become with losing, the easier losing is."
-Nick Saban

LOSER'S LIMP

Anyone who has competed in sports for any length of time knows what a "loser's limp" looks like. For those unfamiliar with the term "loser's limp," it refers to a player acting out an injury after blowing a big play or losing to a lesser opponent.

We would like to have a dollar for every time we have seen this in sales over the years. Salespeople are like athletes. They have chances to make big sales, but they miss. They then begin to search for an excuse for coming up short.

Looking for an excuse is a much-used way to attempt to save face with others. But deep down the person who uses a "loser's limp" knows better—it was a blown deal. A loser's limp is a great way to lose the respect of your peers, notably when it becomes a consistent occurrence.

We all fail to execute on occasion. Yet, if something on the outside is always blamed when things go off track, there is little desire or ambition to address the internal challenges. How about you? Do you search for a crutch when you come up short?

To use the ready-made excuse of a "loser's limp," never changes the outcome. It never makes things better, either. It has been our experience that the further up the success ladder you climb the less you will find the need to use a "loser's limp" as an excuse for poor results.

The rule is simple: *"If you mess up, fess up."* You can never find a solid rung on the success ladder if you spend time searching for excuses. To move on beyond a "loser's limp," ask yourself this question: "What am I doing about the one thing I can improve: *"What am I doing about me?"*

**Experience is what we gain when we take
something from failure that leads to success.**

Nothing inhibits progress more than making excuses and passing the blame. The moment an individual searches for an excuse--any excuse for a loss--is the moment that person limits their possibilities for future success. Relying on excuses for shortcomings does nothing to change or improve those faults. Please understand that the further up the success ladder you hope to climb, the less you will search for—and make-- excuses for poor performance.

HEADS...UP

So, you lost. Got the stuffing knocked out of you, did you? What is your normal posture after you experience a tough loss? Head down with shoulders slumped, right? The head position is body language personified. Here is a great reminder: *"Let me see your eyes."* With head raised, you only see what is happening now.

Do you realize it's mentally impossible to walk around with your head up and eyes open and think negative thoughts? You must drop your head or even close your eyes to think negatively.

Every emotion has its corresponding physical counterpart. Something remarkable happens when you lift your head, square your shoulders, and stand tall. These very physical acts trigger biological processes that alter the mind's perception of what it is "supposed to feel." Your mind shifts toward more positive thoughts, and you start to cultivate positive feelings.

Keep your head up and your eyes level when things are not going your way. This simple act will help you focus on what lies ahead. It will keep you focused on doing your best right where you are. You will make more remarkable strides when your head is up, and your eyes are open.

FIVE MINUTES

As a manager/broker of a real estate office, I (Jim) told those agents who felt sorry for themselves that they had five minutes to feel as sad and miserable as they wanted to. I would set a timer for those five minutes. After that, they were expected to return to their normal business activities.

They usually laugh with me as they quickly understand my point. I also ask them, *"Five or six months from now, do you think anyone will remember this issue?"* The answer is typically NO.

> *You cannot go back to where you failed and make a new beginning...but you can start where you are with a new beginning and make a new ending."*
> -Stephen Covey

SUCCESS GIVES CLUES

This chapter highlights the importance of learning from the lessons arising from defeat. We will conclude this chapter by discussing how experiencing success in sales provides valuable insights for improving results. What must you do to continue climbing the success ladder in the fashion you have demonstrated in the past?

Making sales always has built-in clues as to what must be done to continue along that path. There are lessons to be learned from winning sales, just as there are from losing sales. The key is to look at sales as a building block. You will always find signs in those successful sales that point out ways to help improve the sales process. Look for them and learn from them.

Regardless of how high you are on the success ladder, there are always things to learn that can help you become better. You must continually improve your body of work.

"(Selling) is a competitive event. Always perform in such a way that if you fail to make a sale, walk away feeling like the competition succeeded more than you failed."
-Dr. Marv Levy

Too Soon to Quit

Some have told you it can't be done,
Maybe you have thought them right;
But the time will come to move ahead,
Because somehow you think you might.
In the beginning, losses may be many,
Putting to the supreme test your grit;
But a little voice will say: "Stay with it,
Hang in there, it's too soon to quit!"
So, you raised your efforts a bit higher,
And did what others said couldn't be done;
For you had learned it's too soon to quit,
And with that attitude, by golly you won!   -

Chapter Thirteen

GOALS TO GROW

"A goal is a vision about where you would like to be at some point in the future."
-Jim Rone

Motivation is the key factor behind achieving any significant goal. It can be described as a psychological driving force that arouses or reinforces action toward the desired goal of performing at peak capacity and creating opportunities for success. Both internal and external factors influence motivation.

External motivation plays a significant role in encouraging individuals to take action by offering awards and rewards. Unquestionably, winning the trophy can be a motivating goal. However, internal motivation factors ultimately drive the change.

Internal motivation is a product of our purpose, values, and beliefs. It is the driving force behind seeing just how good you can be. Internal motivation is the only one sustained through tough times and provides external stimuli that affect progress. The strength to become the best arises from internal motivation, where you do not feel the need to depend on outer incentives of any kind to get you going.

Internal motivation is the type of motivation that finds its place in the goals you set for yourself. Motivational goals are immensely personal and rarely rise above the level you set. To soar high, sow big.

Internal motivation tends to work its way over and through goals that may appear uncomfortable to achieve initially. However, once you become immersed in working toward fulfilling those goals, they become even more significant motivators.

Another critical factor in setting motivational goals is whether your chosen entrepreneurial career allows you to utilize your talents most effectively. Are you doing what you enjoy in an environment where you genuinely enjoy it? Your talents should align with your career choice.

SENSE OF PURPOSE

As your goal is, so is your purpose.

As your purpose is, so is your will.

As your will is, so are your deeds.

As your deeds are, so are your rewards.

Do you have a crystal-clear purpose for what you want to accomplish in your entrepreneurial experience? Your path to becoming a superb entrepreneur begins with a solid purpose around which you build your motivational goals. This is the course you take to aspire toward your destiny. Real self-growth does not happen without a solid and realistic purpose.

The backbone of becoming the entrepreneur you aspire to be is a purpose that arises deep within you. Your purpose is already within you. Your role is to uncover it.

With a tremendous underlying purpose, you are more likely always to have direction, your goals are more secure, your focus is razor-sharp, and your potential is more pronounced. With a strong sense of purpose, you quickly and more readily tap into the reserves of energy, desire, and courage. Purpose enables you to connect with your mission and be passionate about it. It sits right at the heart of your soul.

How do you establish a greater sense of purpose? It evolves from doing things that come naturally to you. Can you see opportunities amidst problems? Can you come up with solutions by thinking outside the box? Can you step out of your comfort zone and move beyond the status quo? Are you a natural-born leader? Are you a gifted communicator? Are you a problem-solver? Are you great with people? What are your strengths?

With a true sense of purpose, you will tend to look at yourself--not as the person you are–but as the person you can become. You will never grow beyond the person you are until you decide who you want to be.

MISSION STATEMENT

Think of your purpose as being your mission statement. *"I want to be…I want to do… I want to have…"* The answers hold the purpose for your entrepreneurial experience. The most significant purpose is doing something you can enjoy.

Both of us have mission statements. Jim calls his a Life Mission Statement. Lou's is his Career Mission Statement. Our mission statements look like this:

Jim: *"To help people to do what they do, to do it better!"*

Lou: *"I will do all I can to make the world a better place in which to live through the legacy of doing something that outlives me."*

Joe Tye, one of Jim's mentors, outlined a tremendously innovative technique that helps one remain focused on what they want to achieve, whether great or small. The technique is known as the Direction-Deflection-Question (DDQ) technique. It works well with one's life's mission.

The way it works is very simple. Ask yourself, *"Is what I am about to do leading me closer to achieving my Life's Mission Statement or further away from it?"* If YES, go for it. If NO, stop! The technique is effective for both large and small goals.

> **Establish a quality mission statement, and then the mission statement will help to establish you.**

YOUR WHY

Closely akin to your purpose is your "Why?" Think about the four facets of a life well-lived: **body, brain, heart, and soul**. Do you have a good *"why"* in each of these areas that will highlight why you want to be a successful entrepreneur?

Understanding your *"why"* keeps your desire high and provides the inner drive to keep you going when conditions are challenging. To achieve something great in the entrepreneurial world, clarify your *"whys."*

Your *"whys"* will guide you through the bumps and bruises of business life and help you emerge on the other side as the entrepreneur you desire to be. Write at least ten core *"whys"* of what you want to accomplish in your entrepreneurial career. We recommend that you do this before proceeding. Do it now?

VISUALIZE SUCCESS

> ***"The only thing worse than being
> blind is having sight and no vision."***
> -Helen Keller

Your purpose has at its very core a vision. From this visionary start, you formulate the purpose of what you want to accomplish as an entrepreneur. This vision enables you to develop the entrepreneurial results you want to achieve in your imagination. If you can imagine it, you can do it. If you can visualize it, you can become it.

Since your vision is set at the heart of your purpose, it becomes the centerpiece of establishing goals that take you further than the eye can see. Think about that. It is best to avoid focusing on easily achievable goals. Let your imagination reach far beyond your horizon, where you find *stretch* goals.

The imagination is the workshop where the construction of your future begins. It allows you to explore the possibilities and probabilities that can be created on the road to success. The imagination lays the pavement over which your reality ride eventually carries you.

On your visualized trips, imagine being and doing *something special. Visualize your plan well in advance of beginning* the journey. Imagine what must be done to reach the pinnacle of a triumphant destination. Getting from here to there is challenging if you have no idea where 'there' is.

Following your vision will create an environment where you can grow and improve, as you take active steps to support yourself in this process. It all begins with a vision…, and then you move on to action and reward.

> Entrepreneurial success arises from a vision. It really begins with a statement that loops around your brain, saying, *"I can do this?"* From this visionary start, you move forward to answer the question in your mind's eye with a resounding "Yes!" You will rise above your vision to acclimate yourself to the environment where you grow and improve because you did something to help elevate yourself to new standards.

GOAL-SETTING

> *Goal-setting is like planning a trip: First, locate where you are…decide where you want to go…and third, plan the route to get there.*

"Goals provide direction. Where do you want to be after you have gone through a series of sales experiences? Know where you are headed is crucial to the success of these experiences."
-Jill Korrath

GOAL-SETTING KEYS

- Goal setting is done from the future back to the present. Learn from yesterday, plan for tomorrow, act your best in the present.
- Set realistic, challenging, daily, weekly, and seasonal goals that are desirable, believable, and achievable.
- Always begin your goal-setting statements with the term, "*I am...I will...I can...*" Consider what the action will look like as you work toward your end goal.
- Set stretch goals, but don't set them so high that they are rarely accomplished. Goals that extend beyond the grasp have the best motivational value over the long run.
- To be effective, goals must be measured in terms of quantity, quality, and time. Otherwise, they are probably not worth the time spent identifying them.
- Write your goals down so you can see them...study them...refer back to them. This not only gives you a chance to check up occasionally to determine the extent of your progress, but it also creates focus, and what you focus on tends to expand.
- Goals to be reached must harmonize with action. In other words, goals are achieved through daily action plans and proper execution.
- Identify the obstacles that must be overcome to achieve your goals. Then, plan what you need to do to overcome those obstacles.
- Goals should be shared with those who can provide encouragement and assistance in achieving them. Getting them involved also reaffirms a personal commitment.
- Set a deadline for each goal. Some goals may have natural deadlines–the length of time, etc.- but if they don't, set them. Without time deadlines, goals are limited in value.

ANNUAL-MONTHLY-DAILY

Begin with the end in mind. What will your business look like a year from now? Once you establish where you want to be a year out, do some reverse engineering to define precisely what you must achieve each day to reach your desired results. Here's an idea that has worked for us.

Outline your annual goals. You should set your yearly goals by categories: Financial, Sales Numbers, Physical, Spiritual, Family, and Health. Take the financial goal for example. Use $120,000 as an annual income goal. That means you would have a monthly goal of $10,000 and a weekly goal of $2500. Then you outline precisely what you must do daily to keep yourself on track to achieve your goals. How many contacts, connections, sales interviews, and sales are needed to reach your daily financial goal?

Keeping your focus on what you need to do daily will enable you to achieve your monthly and annual goals. Break the whole down into parts. It's a simple but great system to follow.

The same principles work for any other goal you want to achieve. Need to lose a few pounds? Establish your goal by using the same system. You may not need an annual goal. Exchange weekly for annual. Here again, have a system to follow. Find one that fits you.

OTHER THOUGHTS ON GOALS

- Goals help capture the desire to extend beyond those limits that you thought possible.

- If you have no idea where you are going, how will you know when you arrive?

- Goals are born in the heart and mind... and only there will they ever die.

- Your number one goal should be to work harder on improving yourself than on anything else that you do.

- Don't establish a goal just to test the waters…set it to make a big splash.

- Don't worry about trying to get ahead of others…the thrust behind your goals should be to stay ahead of your prior performance levels.

- What you get by reaching a goal is not as important as what you become by achieving a goal.

- If you're not setting goals to improve, the chances are good that you're about as good as you're going to get.

-The first two letters of GOAL are GO-

"Goals help capture the desire to extend beyond those limits that you thought possible."
-Ken Blanchard

"Individual goals are born in the heart and mind… and only there will they ever die."
-W. Clement Stone

"The road to success is built on a matter of choice… not a matter of chance. If you have no idea where you are going, how will you know when you arrive?
-Mark Cuban

"The road you travel is clearer… your travels are filled with doing more of the right kind of things… the certainty of the destination is greater, when you know where you're headed."
-Dr. Wayne Dyer, Life Coach

Chapter Fourteen

G.O. (GET ORGANIZED)

Your organizational skills help you to see beyond.

One of the highest purposes of entrepreneurship is to be good stewards of your gifts and talents. We have discussed why you need goals along your entrepreneurial trek. Now, we examine how to utilize your time to maximize activities that foster the growth of your sales and marketing skills, establish new connections, and cultivate long-term client relationships.

In every area of your sales life, getting organized — encompassing time management, planning, scheduling, and prioritizing —will help you succeed. These factors create stability and internalize inspiration. Without them, you will struggle to sustain a well-organized marketing plan.

The secret to being well-organized is to have:

- A *plan* to give directions for how to do it...
- A *schedule* to help determine when to do it...
- *Priorities* to determine the most effective use of time.

These are the questions that you should ask yourself as you develop your activity plan:

- Where am I intending to go? Unless I know where I am going, how do I know when I have arrived?
- How do I plan to get there? A solid plan improves the chances of obtaining better results.

A realistic way to end up on the seat of your pants is to always do things by the seat of your pants.

TIME USAGE QUIZ

SCORE: A=AGREE or D=DISAGREE or N=NOT SURE.

_____1. I tend to do things first that provide the most immediate pleasure.

_____2. I tend to do things requiring little time before things requiring a lot of time.

_____3. I tend to do the easiest things before the difficult things.

_____4. I tend to do what I like to do before I do what I need to do.

_____5. I tend to tackle minor jobs before major jobs.

_____6. I tend to do urgent things before important things.

_____7. I tend to work on projects in order of priority.

_____8. I tend to depend on the opinions of others before I act.

_____9. I tend to respond to crises and emergencies without a hitch, but then I have trouble getting back on track.

_____10. I tend to do things I know how to do faster than things do not know what to do.

_____11. I tend to do more unplanned things than planned ones.

_____12. I tend to wait until a deadline is approaching before I act.

_____13. I tend to respond to the demands of others before tending to my demands.

_____14. I tend to do things that are unscheduled before doing things that are scheduled.

_____15. I tend to do things that are "politically expedient" before doing things that advance me.

TOTAL SCORE: A _____ D _____ N _____

WHAT IT MEANS: A total score of A and N of 9 or higher, means you need to improve your TIME MANAGEMENT skills.

Time is money.

USE TIME WISELY

How you manage time is a significant factor in developing marketing factors. Time is the one resource distributed equally to everyone. Each day has the same number of hours, each hour has the same number of minutes, and each minute has the same number of seconds. That's never going to change.

What changes is how these hours, minutes, and seconds are used. The great paradox of time is that nothing is more unequal than its usage. Time is worth nothing. It is how you use your time that gives it value.

Time is also like talent. You cannot create more of it, but you can maximize its use. Spending time more wisely begins with paying closer attention to how we spend it.

PRINCIPLES FOR USING TIME WISELY

What is the most significant waste of time? According to the experts, it is the inability to get—and stay—organized. We will outline some steps to help you make better use of your time by getting organized, regardless of your current level of proficiency.

Clarify objectives. *"What do I need to do to accelerate my sales and marketing development?"* Break each day of the week into three distinct parts: morning, afternoon, and evening. What do you need to be doing in each segment of the day to maximize your time? Remember, as an entrepreneur, your work is wherever you are.

Plan your activities. *"What do I need to do in the immediate future?"* Time management works in reverse—from the future back to the present. Examine what needs to be done, then plan how to achieve it in the most efficient use of time.

Establish priorities. *"What has to be done now?"* Activities need to be established based on IMPORTANCE AND URGENCY. What is essential does not necessarily always carry a sense of urgency.

Organize messages. *"What emails, text messages, etc. are important to do right now?"* Which of these is worth keeping or responding to immediately? Organize your messages with an emphasis on efficiency.

Recognize your most productive hours. When should I make personal contacts? When is my high-energy time?" Determine the hours when you are at your best and attempt to schedule your key appointments during these high-energy periods.

Evaluate each activity objectively. *"How important is this activity?"* Before scheduling any activity, consider how much it will contribute to the value of your daily activities. Ask yourself: *"Will this activity contribute to the results I want today?"*

Combine tasks. *"What similar tasks can I group?"* Concentrate on one important thing at a time, but do multiple, less important things simultaneously. Also, BE FLEXIBLE. "What enormous tasks can I break up into smaller tasks?" is a good question to ask yourself. Divide large projects into smaller, more manageable stages.

Group phone calls. *"Why should I make as many phone calls as possible at any one time?"* This keeps you focused. How many calls you can make quickly will amaze you when calling has your full attention. Another time-saving step is to tell people what time in the day you prefer to be called. This contributes to your ability to get and stay focused.

Learn to say "No." Ask yourself, *"How effective can I say 'No' to nonproductive activities?"* The more you do, the more you'll be asked—and expected—to do. Learn to tactfully say "No" occasionally, mainly to requests with little value. Saying "No" to others on relatively unimportant things is like saying "Yes" to essential things.

Efficiently use spare time. *"Do I efficiently use my spare time?"* Everybody wastes time waiting for someone, sitting in an office, stuck in a traffic jam, etc. Prepare a folder of work to take with you to peruse during waiting time.

Leverage your time. *"What am I doing others can—and should--be doing?"* To have more time to concentrate on your major responsibilities, it is necessary to let others perform their responsibilities. You will probably wonder why you have been trying to do their job all this time.

GIVE TIME-SAVING SIGNALS

Do you give the people close to you, who contribute nothing to your productivity, too much attention that infringes on your time schedule? Some are good at small talk and engage many in a non-productive conversation.

Whenever possible, set time limits for non-productive discussions or visits. While these visits can add value, it is wise to state before a conversation begins that you have only a few minutes to visit.

Timesaving signals would include creating a greater sense of urgency by remaining in a standing position, using body language such as shuffling papers, looking at some paperwork, or moving to the edge of your seat (if you are sitting down) to signal that you are ready to wind up the conversation.

You may end the conversation by saying, *"That about sums it up,"* or *"I really need to make a call."* If the other person has important business to discuss, that is a different story. Then set a new time or arrange another time if the present time is limited.

TAKE TIME TO SAVE TIME

The following list of suggestions can jumpstart activity and time management. Review them thoroughly and identify areas where improvement is most needed.

Take time to set goals. If you don't know where you are going, how will know when you get there? Set daily goals to help you stretch out. Ensure they are just out of reach, not entirely out of sight. (We have said that before).

Take time to plan/organize. One minute of planning saves three minutes of work or replanning. A structured work plan reduces unnecessary and repetitive tasks. It is a response to a need—not an end in itself.

Take time to schedule/prioritize. A schedule keeps you on track by delivering a progressive system of action. Prioritizing helps you decide what you should focus on—what is essential and what is necessary.

Take time to reflect. Time to reflect allows you to separate the wheat from the chaff—the crucial things from the urgent.

Take time to explain things clearly. Make sure the directions for others are clear.

Take time to review your work. How are you doing the things that you should be doing? A thorough review and correction are crucial for achieving high-quality results.

Take time to think. Slow down long enough each day to think about what you are doing...what you want to do...what you should do. This inward journey becomes increasingly more important, and your day becomes busier.

Take time for your family. You will have less than 1,000 weekends to spend with your children before the age of 18. Will you spend time with them or engage in activities that please you?

Take time to do nothing. The busier you become, the more you need to unwind. This ensures you have something left when it is time to rewind up again.

Take time to enjoy the outdoors. Spend some time enjoying the outdoors. *"Health is your greatest asset."*

Take time for spiritual needs. This is very personal. Spend some time being thankful for who you are and what you have. Being grateful never grows old.

MONOTASKING

Are you looking for someone to give you three easy steps to Create a mark improvement in getting organized immediately?

Meaningful change takes time. So, what happens when you do not experience immediate success? Isn't there a tendency to forego the changes you have been working on and, after a few days, slide right back into the same old pattern?

Skills development occurs in stages. It takes time and effort to become good at anything. Focus on improving a single skill and direct your efforts toward improving that single skill. We have labeled this process *monotasking*.

Monotasking is the ability to embrace *"one thing at once."* The optimum for making positive changes in time management comes through the ability to always focus on improving one skill– or even one step in executing that skill--at a time. Then, when you have mastered that step, it will spur you to master the next step. Then the next one…and so on.

How long does it take to develop a skill? Research indicates that it takes approximately three weeks of conscious effort and hard work for the change to take hold. Then, you will need another month to firmly embed it in your mind and make it a part of your daily routine. Stay with it.

At this point, we suggest that you practice patience. The power of patience results from invisible dividends. Time is working for you. Give yourself adequate time to reach your destination. Patience is what you do in the meantime.

When you have a solid change plan that is thoroughly thought out, one where you have considered all the variables, why shouldn't you give it a chance to work?

Consciously refrain from jumping in and making frequent "adjustments." As you proceed with your three-week change pattern, wait as patiently and determinedly as humanly possible for it to work. Patience pays off when upgrades are second nature. If it is important enough, it is worth waiting for.

PLANNING AND SCHEDULING

Planning and scheduling are crucial to success. These two activities should form the basis for almost all processes and activities in your daily affairs. It's essential to examine their use.

Planning and scheduling are interdependent to achieve maximum results. Planning may involve creating a business plan, setting goals for the foreseeable future, or detailing various tasks that need to be done. The focus of the future course of action is planning for the future.

Scheduling involves setting a timeline. While planning identifies what needs to be done, scheduling determines when these tasks should be completed. Scheduling focuses on specific dates and specific timeframes.

ROLE OF PLANNING AND SCHEDULING

- FOCUS ON THE "NOW." Living in the past is fixated on what you or others have done to you, rather than on what you can do right now.

- THINK THINGS THROUGH. Consider the alternatives available and the consequences of each action.

- BE SPECIFIC IN YOUR NEEDS. What do you want? Let those around you know about specific, legitimate needs. Don't keep others guessing.

- EXAMINE ASSUMPTIONS. Explore possibilities and carefully examine the answers. Use patience.

- GO AFTER YOUR BELIEFS. You do not do what you know, you do what you believe about what you know.

PLANNING AND SCHEDULING BENEFITS

Planning and scheduling lay out the *what*, the *how*, the *why*, and the *when*. The benefits of both are manifold:

- Provides time awareness.
- Increases control of direction.
- Goals are more achievable.
- Prepare in advance what to do and when to do it.
- Helps to react reliably and quickly to change.
- Helps maintain consistency.
- Keeps costs down.
- Unexpected events are handled with minimal delays.
- Works effectively under pressure.
- Pinpoints areas that show potential trouble.
- Progress is easier to track.
- Defines strategies within a realistic framework.
- Helps broaden the field of required actions.
- Provides confidence—you know where to begin and where you are heading.

PRIORITY MANAGEMENT

One of the great time management lessons is to learn how to prioritize. These suggestions make priority decisions better:

- Set your priorities—don't let others set them.
- Make a daily "Things to Accomplish" list.
- Work from your "Things to Accomplish" list.

- Keep your "Things to Accomplish" list simple.

- Break larger or long-term tasks into manageable parts.

- Differentiate between urgent and important tasks.

- Make definite appointments—confirm and keep them.

- Group and perform related tasks together.

- Plan realistically for anything worthwhile takes longer than expected.

- Establish activities based on IMPORTANCE AND URGENCY. *"What is important is seldom urgent, and what is urgent is seldom important."*

- Don't forget to use the 3 R's: Rest, Relaxation, and Recreation to stay balanced. Unsuccessful people often can't wait to escape from their unfulfilling lives, whereas successful people use downtime to recharge their batteries for the challenges ahead.

SET YOUR PARAMETERS

When it comes to prioritizing, it is crucial to set your parameters regarding family and work, and it begins with the cell phone. Explain to your customers how you work, that you return all calls, text messages, and emails, but not necessarily within moments or seconds of receipt.

The best way to emphasize this principle is to put your cell phone away when meeting with a customer and turn it off clearly. You want your customers to feel they are the most important person(s) in the world at that very moment, and you do not wish to be disturbed by a phone call or message.

It is important because you also turn your phone off when you are with family in "family time" and then tell them that you know they understand. It is just important to say to them you will return their call, text message or email as soon as possible. Then ask, *"Will that be okay with you?"* Prevent a potential problem from becoming a reality.

PRIORITIZING: THE "THINGS TO ACCOMPLISH" LIST

You may call this a "TO DO" list. We refer to it as a "THINGS TO ACCOMPLISH" list. Evaluate the activities on your "Things to Accomplish" list based on their relative importance. The following questions help prioritize your daily tasks onto your "Things to Accomplish" list. Ask yourself:

- What are my top priorities to accomplish today?
- Which will give me the best return for the time invested?
- Which tasks can I do that no one else can?
- Which tasks, if left undone, will pose the greatest threat to my progress?
- Which tasks do I consider most essential to making progress today?
- Which incomplete tasks from previous days need to be done today?
- Which tasks can I get help with to complete ASAP?

STARTING AND STICKING WITH PRIORITIES

- Be flexible…evaluate your priorities and adjust your course accordingly.
- Do what must be done when it must be done.
- Visualize yourself completing a task... and vividly see the rewards *you* will receive.
- Avoid pessimists…they discourage you from even trying.
- You don't have to be perfect—just excellent.
- Mistakes reveal what works and what doesn't.

Here's a recommendation for you. Use a red pen to indicate an item has been accomplished on each task on your *"Things To Accomplish List."* Keep your past Daily *"Things To Accomplish Lists."* Whenever you feel like you're in a rut and not achieving the success you'd like, review your old lists and look at all the red detailing what you have accomplished, which helps eliminate the fear of failure.

ORGANIZING THOUGHTS

Do you struggle to organize your thoughts? If so, take these suggestions to heart:

- **Scrutinize what you hear.** Be cautious about adopting someone else's opinion and making it your own, as it may sound convincing. Scrutinize, question, or test it before you accept it.

- **"Will it work?"** Brilliant revelations bouncing off the walls of your mind are only sufficient if they can pass the application test.

- **Practice discernment.** Carefully discern the information you receive. Practice defining what will be helpful to and what will not. Filter out those that do not apply to your people skills mission.

- **"I don't know."** If you don't know, say so. To say 'I don't know, is a sign that you know what you know, and you also know what you don't know."

- **Ask questions.** There is no such thing as a dumb question …but you may get or give a dumb answer. Please don't pretend you know something when you really don't understand it. Ask to be sure.

- **Classify information.** Computers and electronic storage make it easier to classify personal thoughts. They enhance recall abilities.

- **Learn to brain map.** When an electronic device fails to work and you have several tasks to attend to, consider the number of things to be done. *"I have these five things to do."* Using a number will map out a strategy for your brain and aid your recall ability.

- **"Proprietor of useless information."** Waste little time in acquiring "useless" general information that you could look up on the internet at a moment's notice.

- **Read and study with a purpose.** Rarely do I read anything without taking notes on a pad or my computer. Have the purpose of learning in mind when reading.

- **Make learning your daily companion.** What information will be beneficial today? You don't know all you need to know about what you should know. Continue to push the learning curve forward.

- **Pay close attention to your thought process.** Your thoughts will be the basis of mostly what happens to you.

- **Keep your thoughts positive**. Ultimately, this will make the most incredible difference in the effectiveness of your thoughts when applied. An upbeat thought process may not make an impression on everyone, but it will on most people you contact. The better your attitude when interacting with others, the greater your influence in their lives will be. This is redundant for emphasis.

PREPARATION HABITS

Preparation habits are crucial to entrepreneurial success. To sit back, hoping that a bit of action here or there will be the magic pill that leads to more excellent production, is the epitome of disappointment. To change reality, preparation sits front and center in making quality adjustments in how improvement occurs. You do what you are prepared to do.

A rush of deliberate and continuous action in the preparation phase of anything triggers the drive toward successful results. Growth in sales and marketing skills depends on intense and directed efforts to expand your attention to being better prepared. Mechanics, techniques, and tactics rely on a full-blast preparation effort. Every opportunity presented offers a path to developing new relationships and new business.

The key is to take control of your preparation time to prepare more effectively. With better control, you establish a solid foundation for greater effectiveness in all that you do.

Preparation may not always bring success,
but there is no success without preparation.

THOUGHTS ON PREPARATION

- It is not preparing for the things you like to do, that will make you more successful; it is preparing for the things you must do to be successful.

- The fundamental theme behind all preparation efforts is constantly moving beyond what you are to achieve the more significant potential of what you can become.

- A priceless performance, one that excels in almost every aspect, will always be preceded by paying the price of preparation.

- Performing at your very best during every opportunity is a matter of what you are willing to do to prepare for that level of performance.

- The only way to improve is to prepare in a way you have never prepared before.

- Prepare to do the right job…right.

- Repetitive preparation is what creates habits. Then those same habits are what creates us.

IMPROVING PREPARATION HABITS

Two habits you must strive to eliminate...

- The habit of placing limits on yourself.
- The habit of letting others place limits on you.

The three stages of habits are:

- Stranger
- Companion
- Master (Good or Bad?)

A great way to improve your preparation habits is to:

- Seek the advice you need to have, not the advice you may like to hear.
- Be willing to attach yourself to those who know what you need to know.

Preparation is crucial to reaching a desirable performance level. You must undergo much trial and error. Establish a pattern of skills you want to improve and design a plan to achieve that improvement. Always be receptive to ideas and information that connect you to a brighter future in sales skills.

MAJOR IN MINORS

Before we close, we want to emphasize the importance of majoring in minors. This is where you plan for all the little things that can make a difference between good and great.

Greatness is not necessarily defined by doing the big things, even though they are essential. Being great in sales is nothing more than a lot of little things done well.

Enthusiastically, stretch out to perform the little things that many would not consider worthwhile. Learn to do the little things before you can do the big things that will make you big.

If you want to make a dramatic impact in sales and marketing, don't be too big to do the little things that will make you big. Never underestimate the bigness of little.

What we mean is that everyday attention to little things is no little thing. Big opportunities are more likely to come to those who make the most of the little ones. Progress is built on doing the little things you may have spent little time doing before.

Do you hear us saying that you will only be as big as you do the little things that are generally critical to success? Never feel too big to plan for the little things that can lead to enjoying life's best moments. Here are some additional reminders:

- Little things make big things bigger.
- You will only be as big as the little things, which will help you focus on the essential things.
- Champions do the little things without being told to do them… and keep doing them.
- Achieving something great is to encounter and overcome all the small things that contribute to greatness.

You need structure in your daily activities to take consistent steps forward. Your brain functions more efficiently when your activities are organized. Put another way, organizing your activities organizes your thought patterns. Being organized puts you in a better position to assess and measure your daily activities and their alignment with your purpose and goals. Motivation is more straightforward when you know what you want to do and how to accomplish it.

Time is worth nothing in and of itself.
It is how time is used that puts a value on it.

Chapter Fifteen

WHAT HOLDS YOU BACK?

To create a more abundant and fulfilling entrepreneurial future, one must answer two questions: *"What fears are holding me back from reaching my goals? What must I do to move beyond the fears that I may be experiencing?"*

Experts tell us that fear is often at the forefront of the lack of achieving more tremendous entrepreneurial success. Someone said that "F.E.A.R. is an acronym for F.alse E.xperiences A.ppearing R.eal." This is an excellent description of fear. This quote from an unknown source has the ring of truism wrapped all around it.

Experts also tell us that we are born with only two innate fears: fear of loud noise and fear of falling. This means all the other fears and phobias we experience are learned.

There is little question that fear plays a more significant role in the inability to interact and interface with probable customers than most entrepreneurs care to recognize. These fears become so real that they emerge as explicit and deeply ingrained behavioral characteristics. There is no question that fear is a fundamental factor in the sales process for many entrepreneurs. Fear often holds aspiring entrepreneurs back from reaching their full potential.

Whatever the cause, when fears have a foothold, they not only tend to diminish but also intimidate and debilitate who we are and what we stand for. Fear can ultimately distort our perception of ourselves and impair our ability to engage others in a crucial discussion about what we offer for sale.

ORIGIN OF FEAR

Fears are experienced from infancy to adulthood. Infancy fears typically stem from a reaction to regular occurrences in our environment. As we grew older, these fears broadened and intensified to encompass a broader range of people, imaginary figures, objects, and events.

Those internal fears originated over time and eventually took root in the psyche. Because they originate in the mind, it is not the fears that are the biggest concern, it is the thoughts created by the fears that one experiences.

For example, no one fears heights; they are so scared of falling. No one is afraid to try something new, they are fearful of the unknown that comes with it. No one is afraid of praise and adoration; they are afraid they won't live up to it the next time.

No one is afraid to seek the conversion of a connection to a prospect, they are worried they won't like themselves if they are unsuccessful. No one is afraid to ask for a "Yes" to their offer, they are afraid to of receiving a "No." No one is afraid of the future; they are scared of what it holds. No one is afraid to reach out and touch someone, they are afraid they will not be touched back.

As you can see, fears develop from illusory thoughts that become real over time. The longer we hold onto fears, the deeper and broader their roots grow. They become ingrained in our psyche and can become so legitimate that they become an actuality in daily sales activities.

FEARS NAMED

How we visualize fear has a significantly greater impact on any situation than the fear itself. Although fearful thoughts and feelings arise from something specific occurring in the present, they often echo past experiences. They also arise from anticipating or expecting a future threat, regardless of how real they are to us.

We want to discuss five fears with you in the rest of this chapter. These are 1) Fear of Success; 2) Fear of Failure; 3) Fear of Rejection; 4) Fear of Loss; and 5) Fear of Intrusion.

FEAR OF SUCCESS

Here are a couple of straightforward questions for you. Do you feel that you are sometimes your own worst enemy? Do you tend to sabotage opportunities for greater success in your life?

Some entrepreneurs create snags of their own making. They believe they should not be, or have not earned, the right to be successful. Consequently, they find a way to sabotage any potential success they experience. Just about the time they find themselves on the verge of being successful, they stick a pin in it.

Take me (Jim), for example. In the 1960s while I was in High School, my father constantly told me, *"If you don't go to college you won't amount to anything."* He was trying to instill in me the desire to attend college and the importance of furthering my education. He was doing what he thought was right. I went to college but did not finish. The seeds of *"You won't amount to anything without a college education"* had been sown.

Throughout my early work life, until I was in my forties, I progressed along a career path, and then it would happen. When the future looked brighter at what I was doing, I would stop and make a change. It was a classic case of Fear of Success.

It was not until someone pointed out the facts of this fear to me, that I recognized the problem. Becoming aware of how restrictive those words were at age 14-18, was the impetus to do something about it. The fear was much easier to understand and change. I put it behind me and had a great career in real estate.

Are you prone to letting the opinions and suggestions of others determine whether you are successful or not? Have you ever thought about how much of your time is spent thinking about how you fear people-related things—like the opinions of others you cannot control?

The opinions of others create mental entanglements that weigh on your ability to gauge what success is. What others say about you can lead you to experience unreal expectations. Those opinions influence your perception of achieving a level of success that you can enjoy.

Your ability to impact your world depends on how you learn to control your thoughts about the opinions of those you might have let affect your level of success. When you release yourself from being consumed by pointless concerns over what others say, you will make consummate strides in appreciating your success.

Be aware that you may not achieve the success you want because you won't allow yourself to have it or don't feel you deserve it. If the fear of success is challenging for you, you will find something in this book that will propel you to move on beyond that fear. See yourself enjoying all the great success you will experience in the future. When you earn it, you deserve a pat on the back.

FEAR OF FAILURE

The fear of failure can affect people in various ways, making it challenging to identify. People often have different definitions of what failure means. For some people, it means not achieving something exactly as they planned. This can create a set of expectations that is very difficult to meet.

The fear of failure can also be present when we miss out on a prime opportunity rather than face the possibility we might fail and enjoy little or no success. No one likes to fail, but it is not uncommon to find people who refrain from taking a risk rather than face the possibility that their attempt may fall flat.

Here are some other reasons why entrepreneurs experience the fear of failure:

- Believing they lack the skills or knowledge to achieve a higher level of success…

- Feeling like they won't be able to achieve their goals…

- Procrastinating to the point that it affects performance or ability to finish on time…

- Telling people that they will probably fail so that expectations remain low…

- Underestimating abilities to avoid feeling let down…

- Distressing that they will disappoint others if they fail…

- Worrying that imperfections or shortcomings will make others think less of them…

The fundamental origin of the fear of failure is the desire for perfection. The challenging willingness to show others that you can be perfect stems from the erroneous expectation of perfection. Those who expect perfection tend to spend significant time thinking up excuses for why things get off track or searching for ways to cover up their mistakes. Failure, as a word, has a meaning familiar to the person experiencing it.

Perfection is something to strive for, but somewhere along the way, it is crucial to compromise with the desire to be perfect. What you try to do and fail at doesn't generate the most significant regret—it is not attempted at all because of the fear of being less than perfect. It is best to read that one again.

There are potential consequences when nothing is done, just as surely as there are possible consequences when you attempt something and fail. Even if you come up short, there is the satisfaction of knowing you gave yourself every chance to succeed. Perfection is not needed to be highly successful. Excellence works wonders in the world of entrepreneurial selling. It is good enough.

FEAR OF REJECTION

This is one of the more prominent fears affecting sales growth. It infiltrates the lives of too many entrepreneurs.

Acceptance is the golden grail that salespeople cherish. The worst thing in the sales world is hearing "No." It arises from a situation where you take the initiative, request an action, and then are told "no" more than once. A classic case of rejection ensues.

The mental game created by this scenario leads to the Fear of Rejection. It originates from the fear of hearing *"No."* A *"No"* can come in many forms and ways, but it always conveys the same message—as a form of rejection.

In a competitive world, there are always rough patches in your attempt to convince others of your way of thinking, join your cause, or follow your directions. Others saying *"No"* means it either deters your efforts to obtain a new customer or allows you to seek another way to experience a *"Yes."*

Often, the most challenging part is finding the strength and courage to move on beyond the "Nos." A solid way to go right through the varied forms of "Nos" is to take the following to heart:

- Some rejection is expected in any role that involves people. Accept that being rejected has happened, happens, and will continue to happen. Once this vital truth is accepted, you can address it on your own terms.

- Don't blame yourself or assume something is wrong when rejected: *"A 'no' to you is not a no about you."*

- People are not rejecting you; they are rejecting an idea, a proposal, etc. Let it hurt a little, then use the power of your *forgettery* again — and get ready to move on beyond the "no" by asking again for a "yes," right?

- What is a *"No"* anyway? Is it an answer? Or a question? Isn't it a question from someone eager for you to extend enough reasons so they can say "Yes?"

- Try to find the basis for the "No." *"You have a reason for feeling like you do. Do you mind if I ask you what it is?"* This can provide the feedback necessary to move things forward.

- Believe in the law of averages—that each *"No"* brings you that much closer to a *"Yes."* Rejection doesn't mean *never* ...it means someone is not ready to accept you into their sphere of influence—yet!

Grasp this vital message: If you never admit to being afraid of rejection, it means you seldom put yourself in a position to be rejected. Ask: *"What is the worst thing that can happen?"* That's right: someone can say *"No."* Please understand the *"Nos"* you hear only become final and fatal when you let them paralyze you from continually seeking ways to get to "Yes."

Social media websites have produced an insatiable appetite for keeping up with peer groups. Are you numbered in this group? This social intervention with peers has brought the fear of loss right into the middle of the picture. This fear that develops from external pressure has two parts: the FEAR OF MISSING OUT, or FOMO, and the FEAR OF BEING LEFT OUT, or **FBLO.**

While closely related, there are distinct differences between the two. Here's a look at those differences. FOMO is a fear of regret that arises from knowing about or having received more or something better than we possess. FOMO is simply an obsessive concern about missing out on important events and material stuff others enjoy. A deep desire to stay connected with the "in crowd" embodies it.

FBLO perpetuates the dread of making the wrong choice and wishing we could have experienced something different. It's a factor of the *"if only"* syndrome. *"If only I had listened to so-and-so, I would have done that and be enjoying..."*

Entrepreneurs who fear they have been *"left behind"* constantly weigh their own experiences against those experienced by others. As a result, their success only counts for them as it relates to others.

What are the costs of these two elements of the fear of loss? Constantly striving to measure up, creating a sales life full of stress and anxiety, being envious, feeling pressured, and experiencing feelings of insecurity offer no pluses for any entrepreneur. The only comparison that should interest you is the one you make between doing better today than you did yesterday and the day before that.

FEAR OF INTRUSION

The fear of intrusion is a hidden shortcoming that ultimately leads us to minimize its negative influence on our sales lives. Because of the lack of specificity about the causes of the fear of intrusion, we tend to relegate it to the far corners of our minds. This is true even when we are consciously aware of the fear itself. There is still a tendency to try to hide it somewhere.

For example, the desire to be liked dominated my (Lou) thoughts early in my entrepreneurial career. This led to my decision to forgo asking close friends and associates to listen to my sales presentations about a product. I did not want to intrude on their lives with a sales pitch. It took me some time to overcome it.

Those who fail to address others and share what they do would prefer to be asked by the potential customer, *"What is it that you are selling?"*

The emphasis is on them first expressing their interest. Even when you are aware of this fear, there is an innate tendency to try and hide it somewhere, probably because you cannot define the origin and the specificity of what caused this fear to develop.

"Out of sight, out of mind" results in facing an unknown future filled with an undefined fear of intrusion. Entrepreneurs who struggle to make a decisive and rational effort to pinpoint why they possess this fear will hold on to it until they decide to face it.

The good news is that whatever fearful beliefs are generated by others, entrenched in your sales life, can be unlearned. If you put too much weight on the concerns of others, this saying is for you: *"Others are too concerned with their own lives to be overly concerned with yours."* You take care of you, and the opportunity for more extraordinary results will ensue.

MANAGING FEARS

Stretching out and expanding your horizons depends on understanding the role of fear in your life and then taking steps to manage it. If fear is covering up the incredible things you could accomplish, employ *"now courage"* and take the steps today to do something about it. That decision belongs to you.

The key is to enhance your ability to face up to and better manage fears. These steps are designed to help manage fears:

Acknowledgment. What is the number one fear adversely affecting your life? Get fired up about taking action. Recognizing what fear is robbing you of experiencing is the first step in managing it.

Evaluation. Attempt to uncover the underlying nature of the fear (or fears) that affect your entrepreneurial life. What is the root cause: 1) you grew up with critics; 2) you have perfectionistic expectations; or 3) you have encountered traumatic experiences? Having a good understanding of what has led to the development of a fear (or fears) is paramount to addressing it. This mindset provides an opportunity to develop the backbone to confront fear. Dissect the fear holding you back and examine it objectively as you explore options to overcome it.

OPTIONS. Establish a game plan to overcome the fear that is holding you back. What options are available to quell it? What tools or methods can help eradicate the fear(s) that are altering your sales life? Explore the reality of the fear(s) you face to learn what options will help you move toward eliminating it.

ACTION. Ralph Waldo Emerson said, *"Do the things you are afraid to do, and the death of fear is certain."* Entrepreneurs who achieve tremendous success in almost everything they do are those who make a meaningful attempt at something, regardless of fear. They are also the ones who occasionally fail to succeed. Despite failure or setbacks, they continue to seek answers to move forward. They learn lessons from their missed opportunities that help them to grow from the experiences. They put their best *efforts to good use and do what it takes to succeed the next time* — and the times after that.

Chapter Sixteen

RISK IT

"Don't worry about failure— worry about the chances you miss when you don't even try. You can only hit home runs if you're willing to strike out."
-Babe Ruth

To become an entrepreneur is to risk ridicule.

To establish big goals is to risk exposure.

To reach out to probable customers is to risk hearing "No.".

To risk making a sale is to risk losing out.

Risk-taking is a real factor in entrepreneurial success. Otherwise, there is a possibility that you will modify your expectations and shift gears to a lower level of achievement. To perform significantly, risk must be taken.

The decision to become an entrepreneur was a risk in itself. Taking measured risks is the price that must be paid to make progress as your business grows. Those afraid to take even minimal risks may avoid the pain that comes to those who attempt something big and fail. They also forfeit the deep-felt sense of well-being that comes to those who extend themselves beyond the ordinary to seek the extraordinary.

Mark it well: to risk not being successful is the price you must pay to have a chance of being successful. Risks must be taken because the most significant risk in entrepreneurship is exercising too much caution. As my (Lou) friend, Bob Taylor, would say, *"You have to be fearless to be a successful entrepreneur."* Bob has been immensely successful with many entrepreneurial start-ups in the forty-plus years I have known him.

Let us ask you a few questions: Did you not fall the first time you stood and tried to walk? You felt like you were going to drown the first time you tried to swim, didn't you? Did you ride a bicycle the first time you sat on the seat and tried to pedal? You missed hitting the ball the first time you swung the bat, right? Did you have the correct answer for that math equation the first time you tried to solve it? Our point is that the norm for most entrepreneurs is to experience some difficult times in their careers.

The history book of business is full of entrepreneurs who had every reason to throw up their hands and walk away, but they didn't. When you work hard and aggressively advance your career, making prudent risk decisions should be a given.

You will definitely do some things wrong at times. However, if you do not take some risks along the way, you will not achieve a more significant measure of success. Some potholes are inevitable on the road to success.

> We all get knocked off our feet at times by something beyond our control. When we do get knocked down, it still falls to each of us to get up. No one is ever a failure by getting knocked down; they only become a failure if they don't get back up—and then do their best to stay up!

IMAGINE

Imagine navigating your entrepreneurial career without encountering adversity or significant obstacles. That might sound good, but we all know it is not realistic. The very struggles you face when a prudent risk fails make you the person you become. If you are not tested or face resistance, how do you grow? Your willingness to face adversity head-on and take the necessary risks to achieve your goals is central to your ability to succeed.

If your fundamental outlook accepts that unusual things of a negative nature are a natural part of growing, this will undoubtedly make you more mentally prepared when adversity does arise. How you view adversity is crucial. Without a certain degree of tolerance and understanding of adverse situations, they can seem endless and never-ending. The more you view, the more they seem to be there.

Murphy's Law says, *"When something can go wrong, a time will arise when it will."* For many, when an adverse occasion arises, it comes as a shock, causing extreme mental distress. The depth of the feelings experienced when things get out of whack depends on how ready we are for it. Even when you feel you cannot survive another thing, hold onto hope. You must believe something better is on its way…and it is.

Plan. Prepare. Risk. Perform. That's the route to being ready for things that can get off track. Spend time preparing for what might go wrong and other unexpected occurrences that can arise when you take a risk. Your mind will be much more capable of handling adverse situations when you do everything possible to acquaint yourself with that possibility. Secondly, mentally, consider adversity a challenge you are always ready to take on.

Adverse situations can arise from what you attempt to do and factors outside your control. It can define you depending on how you respond to it. It can also offer the potential to refine and improve you as you work through it. The key here is not around but through.

> *A real factor in success is the ability to hang on where others tend to let go.*
> *A more significant factor is the ability to hang on when you want to let go.*

Tough situations are a natural habitat for winners.

BE THANKFUL FOR CHALLENGES

Significant challenges and opposition allow your inner qualities to shine, which you may never have known existed otherwise. These challenges will enable you to see what you are made of—to stand up and be counted when it counts.

Through the years, we have had the opportunity to rub shoulders with many great achievers. The one constant we discovered about these champions is that they reached lofty positions by overcoming tough resistance, tangible or intangible. Even when their dreams seemed far from reach, they continued until their intentions were met.

These achievers came to terms with the realization that they had what it took to be at their best when the opposition was the most challenging. They learned along the way to appreciate the opportunities hidden in demanding challenges. Have you considered how to harness tremendous resources from the strenuous opposition you encounter? This opposition produces the soil where you grow your best and provides opportunities for your true potential to shine.

Participation is easy in all areas of life when conditions are favorable and tasks are relatively straightforward. But the true test comes when things get a little arduous. You are probably familiar with the old adage: *"When the going gets tough, the tough get going."* Here's a better one: *"When the going gets tough, the tough are already going."* Sound like you?

FLAWED, BUT KICKIN'

Why is it that we spend considerable time and energy trying to avoid the possibility of making mistakes? To maintain our grip on reality, we must acknowledge that mistakes have occurred and will continue to do so. That's a part of being an entrepreneur. That's a part of growing.

Those who attempt to avoid making mistakes generally are passed up by those who are not afraid to make them. If you are a major league baseball fan, you understand that a batter with a lifetime batting average of .300 is Hall of Fame material. Consider this: a batter who is successful only three out of ten times at bat is considered a rousing success.

The one great lesson from this scenario is how the better baseball hitters handle the failure of not getting a hit. They recognize that the key to their success doesn't lie in the misses; it lies in their ability to be consistent in their approach and not let the seventy percent failure affect the thirty percent success.

One of the most useless ways to spend our time is to be perfect in an imperfect world. It simply won't happen. Like the baseball hitter, we have to learn to live with setbacks along the way. *"Flawed, but kickin'"* is a reasonably good description of entrepreneurs striving for perfection but settling for excellence. They know that perfection exists in rare air.

An associate of Thomas Edison, the master inventor of the light bulb and other incredible innovations, once asked him, *"Sir, do you realize we have made 50,000 mistakes?"* Edison calmly replied, *"No, we've found 50,000 things that won't work."*

We wonder how often we have been told to learn from our mistakes. Consider this for a moment: What will we learn? Like Thomas Edison, we will learn things that don't work, right? Success in many entrepreneurial endeavors stems from a process of elimination. You have to do it first to find out.

THE LEARNING LABORATORY

Let us emphasize again that uninterrupted success is indeed rare. The complexity of a forward-looking life is too great not to expect some risk-taking along the way. You must have the courage to accept that an occasional mistake will occur due to risk. That is the price of progress. If you are afraid of making a mistake, at some point, you will make a mistake.

Being willing to do things wrong offers a learning laboratory to discover what is right. It's not the setbacks you make that will cause you to doubt yourself, but the wrong perception of its value. Every time you stumble, you have an opportunity to learn something. A mistake should not be in vain. It offers you vital lessons that we can use to help you advance. Please don't lose the value of the opportunity to learn.

When a mistake is made and corrected, it is an opportunity to improve and progress. The eraser on a pencil is not there to correct errors. It is there for those *willing* to correct their mistakes. Lessons that wouldn't have existed without the opportunity to live through them are learned.

If you do not experience setbacks along the way, it is a reflection that you are not trying your best to move ahead. It means you are being too cautious. The noted author Tom Peters said, "*If it is worth doing, it is worth doing wrong.*"

You will have the opportunity to correct many mistakes along your career path. To do so, though, you must cultivate a workable relationship with your miscalculations. You must see your mistakes as friends who can benefit learning greatly.

Other thoughts to ponder about mistakes:

- To admit you made a mistake is a sign of strength, not a display of weakness.
- A mistake does not define you...the next chance does.
- Mistakes are reasons for growth, not excuses for quitting.
- You can rest assured that if you are afraid of making a mistake, you will inevitably make one at some point.
- Never admitting to making mistakes can increase the likelihood of making them again.
- Learn from the mistakes of others... your career will not be long enough to make them all yourself.
- It's incredible how there's never enough time to do it

right the first time, but there is always time to do it over.

- Just think about how much trouble you might have spared yourself if you could have had your second chance... first.

- It was Benjamin Franklin who said, "*Those things that hurt, instruct.*" Each mistake is an "instructor."

- Potential is something that we have always possessed. The reality is that we either use it or lose it.

> Hanging tough is cut from the fabric of persistence and woven with perseverance. There are no areas in being an entrepreneur that are immune to this combination…you will go as far as your stay-ability will allow you to go.

NO CHALLENGES...NO GLORY

Significant progress emerges from great challenges.

Here's the big question: How well can you persevere when the going gets tough and the outcome is unclear? Does this type of challenge draw out the very best in you?

Challenges in any phase of athletics offer you glimpses of yourself that you may have never seen before. They give you a chance to see your make-up. They can reveal qualities that you may have never known you possess. Challenges allow you to be better than you have been… if you face them. Even when you feel afraid and overwhelmed, stay the course.

A truism in most of the things that count is that there is no measure of gain without pain... no triumphs without trials... no victories without battles... no peaks without valleys... no glory without challenges. Speaking of valleys, Coach Bobby Bowden reminds us, *"The fertilizer that helps us do our best growing is found in the valley, not on the mountaintop."*

If you have developed strong habits of persistence and mental discipline, you will be well-equipped to face tough challenges with these virtues. If you have prepared yourself to face up to challenging situations with courage and conviction --the chances are good that you will enjoy significant rewards. It is worth noting that the challenges you face and work to overcome today are developing the courage and strength that make tomorrow's challenges easier to face.

"It is easy to conclude that something is over when things look bleak, isn't it? Yet an essential part of developing a champion's mentality is to hang in there when the going gets tough, and success appears out of sight."

-Les Brown

> Trials in any phase of entrepreneurship offer you glimpses of yourself that you may have never seen before. They give you a chance to see what you are made of. They can rush to your aid qualities that you may have never known you possess. Trials give you a chance to be better than you have ever been...significant progress emerges from great trials and challenges.

Chapter Seventeen

LANGUAGE OF SUCCESS

Be careful how you talk to yourself,
because someone important is listening!

One of the first steps in developing solid self-confidence is based on the most straightforward strategy. If you stick with it and use it repeatedly, it will almost certainly help you create a strong, abiding belief in yourself. That simple strategy is to always speak the language of success to yourself.

Talking negatively to ourselves is a prevalent habit. We tend to be our harshest critics to boost our performance. We want to be more efficient and effective today than we were yesterday. However, we are often more demanding of ourselves than our actual circumstances would warrant.

Do you tend to be your harshest critic? Are you more critical of yourself than the circumstances would warrant? Do you try to "motivate" yourself by tearing yourself down rather than building yourself up?

When you talk yourself "down," you tend to focus on what you are doing wrong or feel incapable of doing. As a result, you keep your faults and flaws at the forefront of your mind. You have focused on a negative "you."

In this desire to "motivate" yourself to perform better, you are tearing yourself down rather than building yourself up. Privately, you tell yourself, *"I'm not good at this..."* or *"I'm not good at that..."* And the more you tell yourself you are not good at something, the more convinced you will become. Reality will, in kind, reflect this.

You might say, *"I really don't mean these things I am saying to myself about myself."* Seldom do we really "mean" them. But isn't there an inherent problem here?

Self-talk has a way of becoming a self-fulfilling prophecy. Each time you express a negative statement to yourself; you take a step forward in getting good at being destructive to yourself. **You put poison into your system without much thought as to future consequences.**

When the focus of self-talk is skewed toward the negative, you tend to talk to yourself about what you shouldn't or cannot do. You cannot speak negatively to yourself and expect positive solutions. The mind doesn't work that way. Weigh the possible consequences is a smart move.

SELF-TALK BASE

Your performance as an entrepreneur will always be consistent with your thoughts. And what you think is influenced mainly by what you tell yourself about your abilities to perform and your confidence in achieving results.

It is tough to perform at a high level without the support of self-talk. Action on the outside consistently follows the action on the inside. You probably know that. However, some people continually underestimate the impact of their self-talk on personal success. They fail to engage in accurate and realistic inner conversations, which are crucial for advancing as an entrepreneur.

Is self-talk a concern of yours? Do you tend to talk negatively to yourself? I think you realize the importance of what your "inner voice" is saying. I believe you recognize that you cannot speak with yourself in negative terms and expect affirmative results. If it is something you need to work on, now is the time to establish a plan for improving your self-talk.

I (Jim) recommend putting a Post-it note on your bathroom mirror so you can see it first thing every morning. The note could read: IMPROVE MYSELF TALK. Then, put a brown paper lunch bag on your desk to remind you, *"It's in the bag."* Maybe even write that outside the bag with a black magic marker! Training aids are just that—aids to learn by!

MONITOR YOUR SELF-TALK

Muster as much mental muscle as humanly possible to correct self-talk. This is crucial for maximizing sales-fulfilling opportunities. It takes great focus and discipline to change ingrained self-talk patterns and attitudes. Yet, it is possible to turn the unfamiliar into the familiar.

Changing your self-talk habits begins with monitoring your self-talk. Listen to yourself, notably when facing a tense or stressful situation, often during a complicated or intense sale.

In this process, you are working toward two very different goals: First, learn what situations tend to trigger negative comments. Ask yourself, *"What am I telling myself about this particular situation that is negative and self-defeating?"*

Second, the goal is to effectively change your inner dialogue to fit a more upbeat direction. The "take two" technique in filmmaking is a valuable tool to utilize here. When you slip up and talk negatively about yourself, simply back up and mentally tell yourself to strike it from the record and begin anew.

Being aware of what you say to yourself is the first step in refining your self-talk and cultivating a stronger belief in yourself. Once you take this first step, you are well on making key adjustments to your self-talk patterns. Focus. Focus. Focus. That is the key.

Fueled by the attention of this attentive presence, you improve your self-talk and performance. You may feel strange or uncomfortable talking to yourself differently, but it becomes easier with time. As you do this, be aware that you will shock the old programming in your subconscious mind. It is not accustomed to all those excellent new descriptions it can learn.

Any way you look at it, when you speak positively and upbeat to yourself, everything else takes care of itself. So here is our suggestion: For the next twenty-one days, consciously focus on speaking *"up words."* Tell yourself what is right with you – not what is wrong; what you can do -- not what you can't do…What you want to happen, not what you don't want. Dwell on your "plusses", not your "minuses." Use your enthusiasm and energy to lift yourself, not put yourself down. Make your self-talk a catalyst for something better.

AIDS TO SPEAKING "UP" WORDS

- **Keep a close tab on your "apostrophe tees."** You know the ones I am talking about: can't, won't, shouldn't do, wouldn't do, and don't want to do. The more you use these in a personal sense, the more negative you become. Work to eliminate the apostrophe tees.

- **Don't tie yourself in "nots."** If you persist in using self-defeating statements, they become a self-fulfilling prophecy. Eliminate the "nots": The more you tell yourself that you are not good at doing something, the more convinced you become. Untie these "nots:"

> The can nots…
> The may nots…
> The would nots…
> The do nots…
> The will nots…
> The could nots…
> The should nots…
> The am nots…
> Especially the "I am not…"

- *"What if."* Do you say things like: *"If I were this, I would be better at that;"* or *"If I had that, I would be better at this?"* *"What if"* statements never make you better. In fact, they are success-stoppers. They impede things that lead to success.

- **Get off your *"buts."*** You cannot keep up with the changes around you if "*Yes, but...*" becomes your hallmark. Listen to how many times you tell others all the reasons why you can or will do something, then in the next breath, offer a "but" followed by all the reasons why you cannot. It's amazing how everything before the *but* has little or no significance.

- Here is the positive step. Learn to use the "in the bag" concept. Whatever you want to change or improve, state it in the present tense as if it is an accomplished fact. Make your self-talk, statements like: *"I am...", "I have...", "I do...".* When you use this kind of language long enough and persistent enough, it is ingrained in your belief system.

STATEMENTS TO ELIMINATE

Numerous statements about oneself are used, which add nothing to improving one's life. They tend to take away from the positivity needed when facing a difficult life challenge. These statements would include:

- "If I had only…"
- "It's not fair"…
- "This is too complicated"…
- "Why does this have to be so challenging"…?
- "I have to do that?"…
- "Why is this happening to me?"…
- "Wow, how could things be worse?"

Countless other "negative" statements are used when talking to ourselves. None of the statements like those above offer any motivation to seek solutions. They add to the excuse list. In sports, it is called a "*loser's limp*."

Now, review the list of statements at the top and put a positive spin on each. For example, instead of "*Why is this happening to me?*" Use something like this: "*What is it I can learn from this situation?*" Another one could be, "*How can I make this fair?*" Focus on how you can make it a positive practice.

There is a crucial reason why you must consciously consider what you are saying to improve how you speak to yourself. The "*Subconscious mind*" is listening to every word spoken.

THE SUBCONSCIOUS MIND

Remember that everything good will not happen at a moment's notice. If what the subconscious mind has been hearing has been negative, instant miracles cannot be expected. As the reactive mind, the subconscious tends to be skeptical when the conscious mind proposes a change in thinking and acting.

For example, the subconscious mind will react like this: "*Hold on now, who are you trying to fool with all this positive stuff? I'll believe it when I see it!*" Earlier in a previous discussion, we discussed how it will take about 21 days to make any change a daily, ongoing reality in your life.

It will take those three weeks for all the positive thoughts planted in the subconscious mind to be awakened. Then the subconscious one day will say, "*Gosh, you're right about this positive stuff...and I like what I'm hearing.*" Okay. That's probably a stretch, but the result isn't.

To be habitually successful, keep talking with yourself positively and upbeat. Repeat positive, uplifting affirmations to yourself long and powerfully enough so that they eventually register in the far recesses of the subconscious mind. Do it for you.

Chapter Eighteen

WATCH YOUR MORAL COMPASS

Ensure that in living with yourself,
you are in living in good company.

Listen carefully to these words from an unknown source:

"Watch your **thoughts** for they become **words**...
Watch your **words** for they become **actions**...
Watch your **actions** for they become **habits**...
Watch your **habits** for they develop **character**...
Watch your **character**, for it defines your **reputation**."

What is your reputation in the daily environment where you spend most of your time? What is your level of trustworthiness among your customers? Are you doing things right because it is right? It is an impeccable character that leads to building a reputation as an entrepreneur, which makes you more valuable to the outside world.

Character and reputation will make you—or break you—in sales—and life. Character is the mental and moral qualities that are distinctive to your inner substance. Reputation is based on opinions of what others think you are—your public image.

A reputation is a belief that grows and travels by word of mouth. Reputation is a fragile thing. It can be easily fractured if you compromise on the principles of character.

There is little question that your above-board expansion in the world around you is highly dependent on character—on what you are inside. The events of daily sales life not only build character, they reveal character.

Upstanding character is the only sound foundation for a firm reputation. Reputation is like a shadow. Wherever you go, it follows. It cannot be disguised, hidden from, or left behind. It is present 24/7.

What is the status of your reputation? The wise decision is to recognize that you have the potential to establish an even stronger reputation. This is based on the person you are becoming. It takes a long time to develop an immaculate reputation; the history books are full of those who have learned that it can be decimated almost instantly.

Reputation is more than the result of actions alone. Talking one way and acting another can betray trust. Conversations in a sales situation can be open to interpretation, and the words used to shape your proposal can be collectively misunderstood or viewed through tainted perceptions. The moral is that what is said counts in building a reputation. Never lose sight of that fact.

Sitting at the forefront of reputation should be efforts to incorporate the character traits of trust, integrity, and honesty. These attributes reside at the very heart of an unyielding sales platform. An in-depth look at these factors that form the backbone of character and take center stage in developing a solid reputation deserves a closer look. We begin with trust.

TRUST

Words alone cannot convince someone to trust you. Trust is earned, not conveyed. A significant factor in building trust is to strive for a more perceptive awareness of what potential buyers desire in a meaningful sales and marketing relationship. By establishing a platform of deeper understanding, communication with others is broader and more definitive. Your aspiration to know buyers on a more personal basis shines through.

The word "understand" means the ability to stand under. Trust emerges from a more profound understanding established by first being trustworthy yourself. Understanding creates a remarkable atmosphere for the development of trust. It indicates that you are driven by something more vital than personal gain.

Trust is the unyielding base on which relationships with customers flourish. The more they trust what is said and heard, the more open they become to you. Reciprocal behavior lies at the heart of trust. It creates a feeling in your customers that they and you are in it together. And you are.

Honoring the right things enhances your status in the eyes of present and future clients and probable customers. Trustworthiness improves the depth of your relationship with them. Spend time doing things that enrich your personal moral compass values to enhance your value for others. That's a great place to be.

Everything done in social circles depends on trust. Potential customers often start with preconceived notions about you or your company due to its reputation. However, trust becomes the hallmark when it is actively nurtured and continually reinforced in all your dealings with customers.

> *"Potential buyers will find a reason to connect*
> *if they trust you...they will find an excuse not*
> *to connect with you if they don't trust you."*
> -Jim Britt

INTEGRITY

Integrity is another staple of a noble character. Always functioning within the confines of a societal and personal code of morality will establish you as a just and right entrepreneur.

Integrity is something that cannot be forged. Nor can one borrow, buy, or steal it. Like the markings ingrained in the very heart of a tree, integrity is fostered and made palpable by what's on the inside. Integrity functions inside out.

Integrity is earned by consistently demonstrating, through words and deeds, that upholding a moral standard is a higher priority than what can be gained without it. It cannot be achieved in sporadic acts of doing the right thing to satisfy the conscience at any moment. It is doing what is ethically correct, regardless of whether it is noticed or acknowledged. Doing the right thing sometimes may not be popular, but it is right.

If unchecked and undisciplined, ambition can lead to highly unethical practices. To attain a higher level of sales success, a compelling compromise must sometimes be found, but not to the point of prohibitive cost. The secret is to strive for balance and ensure that integrity is left intact, and not used as a bargaining tool.

When released from the things in life that lower internal values, the natural movement is toward higher-level values. Every day, sales-related situations arise, presenting challenges to make right or wrong, good or bad, just or unjust decisions. Most of these situations are routine, while others are unique, and some are particularly important. Almost every choice and action taken in these situations is rooted in integrity.

One of the most demanding forms of mental toughness is deciding what you can live with tomorrow, not what you might get away with today. This requires constantly calibrating a mindset that continually and consistently maintains the fiber of integrity.

The marvel of integrity is that it can be developed and nurtured. It begins with having a clear picture in mind of the quality entrepreneur you want to be—and then acting consistently according to that image. It requires a focused and disciplined approach at all times.

What is the number one thing brought to a relationship with a probable customer? It is the best *you*. Probable customers want to be involved with someone who is authentic and exudes confidence, a person of integrity, a person who feels good about who they are. The infinite truth of what you are is evident. Potential customers will line up to connect with you due to your integrity.

HONESTY

Be honest with yourself... otherwise, you will miss the best part of you.

Honesty can be challenging to discern in a society that has placed confusing and conflicting demands on its value system. The best way to navigate this complex network and level the playing field is to remember that being "almost right" is still wrong. That's the reality of it. Controlling how customers and clients perceive a situation is impossible, but the choice is yours in how you react and address its existence. Be consistent and uncompromising in matters of right and wrong.

Do you know where honesty begins? It begins with being genuinely honest about yourself. Being honest about yourself fosters a clear understanding of who you are and what you stand for. That's a great place to be.

When you are honest about your failings and shortcomings, you put yourself in a position to address them. However, continuing to hide them perpetuates a lie to yourself, without hope of ever coming to terms with why you are not where you would like to be in your entrepreneurial development. This shines through to your customer base.

We realize as much as anyone that being honest and truthful with yourself is difficult. It is a downright problematic chore. Yet, it is essential to do this to look at yourself honestly and improve who you are.

Honesty is the best policy because it significantly affects your relationships with potential customers. Honesty encompasses all the topics we have discussed up to this point. How do you know when your reality of honesty is out of line with actual reality? Again, this is often difficult to discern in a society that places confusing and conflicting demands on our value system.

We feel the best way to negotiate this complicated network and level the playing field is to occasionally remind yourself being *"almost right"* is still wrong. Honesty is an all the time thing, not a some of the time thing.

You cannot control how others perceive situations, but you can choose to control how you respond to and manage them. This choice has a profound impact on your level of honesty.

Do you strive to be truthful with every customer you interact with? Stand firm on the level ground of truth with everyone, everywhere you are.

Here are some reminders about truth with a twist of wit:

- Truth doesn't hurt...unless it ought to.
- Don't stretch the truth...it might snap back.
- Telling the truth diminishes the need for a great memory.
- *"Better to suffer for the truth than to be rewarded for a lie,"* is a great old proverb.
- The truth may be expensive, but in the long run, it is affordable.
- Beware of a half-truth...you don't know which half you will end up with.
- Truth never wobbles. If the truth needs crutches, it is not the whole truth.

We can confidently say that the day of reckoning comes for those who have a problem telling the truth. An ancient saying goes: *"You can fool some people sometimes, but you can't fool all the people all the time."* The truth eventually surfaces.

CHOICES AND CONSEQUENCES

The choice/consequence equation is fundamental in daily entrepreneurial life. We were unsure where it should be placed in the book, but it is at the core of your character's development and reputation. A rule of life states, *"For every choice, there will be a consequence for better or worse."*

Success in the field of selling finds its footing in choices and consequences. The nature of our choices determines the results of everything we do. Some choices carry more weight than others, but no choice is inconsequential in sales—or in life.

Every primary choice made leads inexorably to either advancement or regression. We do not sit still; we do not remain the same. In a broader sense, we either strengthen or weaken the overall situation of the related activities.

When we get right to the heart of many sales situations, we must make some choices about the options presented to us. Whatever the choice, it will have a consequence—an outcome.

To be successful at anything begins with your attitude—with what's inside of you, not what's around you. As an inside-out proposition, you cannot always change what goes on around you, but you can change your thoughts about what is happening around you. You can choose where things improve because you took action to enhance them. You can adjust your attitude to create a favorable environment for success and achievement.

Embrace the concept of choice and consequence in your life and work. Deeply ingrained in your psyche should be the understanding that every choice has consequences. Some of these choices, as mentioned earlier, are inherently more meaningful than others in the broader context. Do not lose sight of the fact that the consequence determines what happens; the choice sets the table.

The consequences will instinctively differ as you gain more experience and make better choices. Repetition—the proper repetition—leads to more quality choices. This, in turn, will lead to more practical and solid consequences.

We want to bring another scenario of choice and consequence to your attention. Each morning, when you wake up, you face two opposing decisions. You can choose to start the day in an upbeat mood, ready to tackle the day on your terms, or you can choose to be negative with a mood that foresees a day full of dullness and drudgery. You do have a choice.

As the day unfolds, you have the choice to react to the things happening around you and within you. This is a substantial reason to understand why it is essential to upgrade your choices to improve the consequences accordingly. The best wisdom in the world is that which keeps you from getting into situations where you need wisdom.

A positive thought process leads to a positive outcome. Study after study has shown that people from all walks of life who make positive, optimistic choices live longer and healthier...have more energy...make better decisions...enjoy superior performance ...are more productive overall...are less stressed...are happier ...have more quality relationships...and have more success in their careers than do those who tend to make pessimistic choices. That is a given.

Please understand that each time something negative occurs during the day, you have a choice: you can choose to do nothing and accept your fate, or you can weigh the options and direct your search toward a positive solution. You do have a choice. Spend the necessary time choosing wisely.

Chapter Nineteen

MANAGING EMOTIONS

"Don't let your emotions be your decision-maker,
leave the emotional decisions to the customer."

Do you allow others to evoke a strong emotional reaction in you? Do you tend to lose your temper with others when things don't go your way? Do you fly off the handle when someone does or says something that you dislike? Do you quickly become angry with yourself when you are not performing as well as others expect you to perform? Unless you maintain a firm grip on your emotions, you can be carried further and further away from the mainstream of enjoyable and successful experiences. Keep in mind that your emotions are that important.

Most of us would like to think that reason and sound judgment dominate our daily affairs. However, almost everything we do is interpreted at the emotional level. In a very real way, we see and react to things through the lens of our emotions.

The word "emotion" comes from the Latin word "exmovere," which means "to excite, stir up or to move." Emotions are a basic and essential part of life—and sales.

One of the most impressive aspects of high-achieving entrepreneurs is that they generally exhibit solid emotional control. While they experience the depth and breadth of a life of emotions, they have a really good handle on them. They have an element of consistency that brings balance to their emotional lives.

This doesn't mean they always refrain from having negative emotional moments. However, they experience them but don't let them take over – they don't dwell on them. They deal with them and then move on to more constructive feelings.

Entrepreneurs who experience success in high-pressure situations do not become overly stressed. They are calm and at ease, which helps them maintain equilibrium in pressure-cooker-type situations. They exercise composure in situations where constraint is vital to performance.

I (Lou) recently read an article that declared a high emotional quotient (EQ) will move one up the success ladder as quickly as a high IQ. It is great to have both, but individuals with broadly developed entrepreneurial personalities who regularly interact with people tend to display great emotional control and stability in their interactions with customers from diverse cultures.

As you probe your own experiences, what can you say about the role emotions play in your life? How are you doing in the areas of emotional control and stability? Are your emotions working for or against you? Are your emotions your best servant or your worst enemy? Are they?

Have you ever considered how much time you spend getting emotionally invested in things you cannot control? There is a tendency to get stuck in mental entanglements with what someone else is doing or not doing, with what others think or say about you, with unreal expectations that others create, with what has happened in the past, and with what might happen in the future. How much control is available over any of these things?

Your overall success will depend on how you learn to focus on the one thing you should always have control over—the power over yourself. When you release yourself from being consumed by pointless concern over what you cannot control, haven't you created room for wholly engaging with what you can control—with those situations and events that will be more meaningful?

You are your emotions, and your emotions are you!

"IT'S OKAY" ATTITUDE

One of the best ways to maintain emotional control is to adopt an "It's okay" attitude. This attitude is based on the premise that if you can do nothing about a situation, why should you get emotional about it?

One of the most effective ways to maximize emotional control is to adopt an "it's okay" attitude. This attitude is based on the premise that if you can do nothing about a situation, why should you get emotionally involved?

Take some day-to-day concerns. Few of us are immune to the little things that can get under our skin and endanger our emotional well-being. What do you do when the driver ahead of you is daydreaming and causes you to miss a green light, and you are already late for a necessary appointment? Do you blow your car horn and blow your stack? How about the customer who stands you up? How do you react to it? Just let it be okay; you can get upset, angry, or miserable, but that doesn't change a thing. Move on to the next potential customer with a refreshed attitude.

Isn't it really okay for the world to move at its own pace? If you get upset, what have you achieved? Will you let someone else's conscious or unconscious action knock you out of your "It's okay" state of mind?

The first step in overcoming any problem is to view it as acceptable. When we accept our problems as okay, we have positioned ourselves to move beyond them and begin seeking an answer or solution. The goal is straightforward: adapt to the realities of life, regardless of how unfair these realities may seem. An "It's okay" attitude helps us to do that.

A roommate of mine (Lou) in pro baseball often used the term, *"You gotta cooperate with the inevitable."* Learn to go with the flow. Let things be. Cooperating with the inevitable occurs when you establish an 'It's okay' attitude. If you do, you will likely last longer and achieve greater success.

MAINTAINING EMOTIONAL CONTROL

Most emotional reactions result from the opinions and suggestions expressed in customer interactions. The outcome of these interactions is often the determining factor in many emotional responses that arise during a sale.

Emotions come. Emotions go. What happens in between is the question. If an emotional reaction leads to a negative outcome, the aftermath can take you to depths that may be difficult to escape. The price for negative emotions is high.

A primary consideration is recognizing that you deal with individuals, not people, encompassing all the substances that the word "individual" represents. One of the most significant discoveries in developing marketing skills is recognizing and appreciating people as individuals. The healthier the involvement with personal emotions, the more influential the ability to connect with and make a difference to those individuals who will become a part of your customer base.

A key to enjoying sales and marketing wisdom revolves around controlling your emotions. Here are some thoughts that should help you:

- Learn how to keep your equilibrium in all kinds of selling situations.

- Avoid becoming overly optimistic when you experience a high degree of success or overly pessimistic when you fail to enjoy enough success.

- Displaying more emotion to achieve higher success is often overrated.

- Managing emotions through your day-in and day-out activities is an internal decision you make despite all of the things that could knock you off track.

- Learn to check tendencies toward becoming overly emotional in intense emotional situations.

- Exercise composure in those situations where restraint is vital to high performance.

- Balance reason with emotion. Keep your perspective and not give up the spark and excitement you bring to your sales efforts.

- We are more apt to remain calm and collected when restrained in an emotional confrontation.

- Not verbalizing your anger… for with fire in your eyes, all that will come out of your mouth are flames.

- Forget about trying to get even—the more you try to get even, the more uneven your performance becomes.

- Learn to stay within yourself. This doesn't mean you have to be emotionless; you need to know how to manage your emotions effectively during a potential customer interaction.

RELAXATION

Much of relaxation is about letting the sales action come to you.

A key factor in handling emotionally charged situations is remaining calm and relaxed. Relaxation decreases the effects of emotional stress and anxiety on the mind and body.

Some entrepreneurs have had their careers cut short due to an inability to handle emotionally charged situations. Over time, the tension generated by stress and anxiety harmed their bodies. It led to mental exhaustion and various health issues.

We firmly believe that adequately employing relaxation techniques can help you cope with stress and stress-related sales situations. Relaxation at the proper moment may be as crucial to improving performance as any undertaking. Take the time to learn relaxation techniques if you become uptight in certain situations. Do this for a brighter future.

Relaxation is a skill. You can train your mind and body to do it. Learning basic relaxation techniques is straightforward. As with any skill development, relaxation techniques improve with practice and experience.

Before moving on to the techniques, we have two thoughts: First, be patient with yourself. Don't let your effort to practice relaxation techniques become yet another stress source. Second, try another if one relaxation technique doesn't work for you. We discuss three here:

Visualization. In this relaxation technique, you take a visual journey where your focus is on your role and the activity you will be engaged in, not on the results of that activity. The results you want will be there when you clear your mind of excess tension, relax, and visualize successfully performing your role and making all the right moves. This is a good technique to use pre-sale. You may want to close your eyes, sit in a quiet spot, loosen any tight clothing, and listen to some soothing music. The aim is to focus on the present and visualize positive actions. We recognize that your sales environment may not permit this, but utilize visualization to the best of your ability.

Muscle Relaxation. In this relaxation technique, you focus on slowly tensing and then relaxing each muscle group. This can help your awareness of the difference between muscle tension and normal relaxation. Muscle relaxation starts by tensing and relaxing the muscles in groups from your toes way up to your head. You can also start with your head and neck and work down to your toes. Focus on tensing your muscles for about five seconds and then relax for 30 seconds, and repeat.

Deep Breathing. When you feel a rush racing through your body, there is an age-old yet straightforward breathing exercise that can help dissipate mental and physical stress. While the deep breathing technique is typically incredibly beneficial for the body, many see it as a great way to relax the mind, even more so than the body.

You can enhance your relaxation ability by utilizing three dimensions through proper deep breathing. The first lesson is to shut your mouth. Secondly, slowly draw in a good deep breath through your nose. Then, thirdly, exhale slowly through your mouth. The pace and manner of your breathing can enhance your ability to relax in tense situations.

> **"Relax and remember this too shall pass...**
> **Peace of mind holds you in good stead all the time."**
> Dr. Wayne Dyer

KEEP YOUR COOL

Our purpose is not to make light of *"keeping your cool,"* but here are some humorous ideas from various unknown sources:

- The more you grow up, the less you will blow up.
- Flying into a rage always results in unsafe landings.
- Those who are always exploding rarely end up being big shots.
- It's more tasteful to swallow angry words before you say them than to eat them afterward.
- Those who lose their heads are the last to realize it.
- Before giving someone a piece of your mind, make sure you can get by with what's left.
- Think first, not last, when the heat is on.
- Be cautious when shooting from the lip.

EMOTIONAL INHIBITORS

There are over six hundred words that express negative feelings. Consequently, negative emotions are part of life. That is a given in your daily affairs.

Unpleasant feelings are just as crucial as enjoyable ones in helping you handle life's ups and downs. If it weren't for a few negative emotions now and then, you wouldn't enjoy the good ones as much, would you?

Certain situations, like losing a job, going through a divorce, facing monetary issues, or witnessing the death of a loved one, all lead to some adverse reaction. The depth of the response you internalize about negative situations could lead to unhealthy conditions and consequences.

A word of caution: Attempting to suppress negative emotions can backfire and even diminish a sense of well-being. Instead of avoiding negative emotions, recognize and manage them. How you deal with emotions, especially negative ones, has significant consequences.

Emotions come and go, but what happens in between is the question. If you do something with negative consequences, the aftermath could lead you to depths you might find difficult to escape from.

Although positive emotions can be a key factor in attaining and maintaining mental stability, research indicates that effectively managing negative emotions also plays a vital role in overall well-being. If this concerns you, work diligently to develop a strong grasp of overcoming negative emotions.

TAKING LIFE IN STRIDE

As we close this segment, it is worth looking at some things that will help to fight emotional extremes:

- Think realistically. Putting things into perspective reduces stress.

- Manage time wisely. Controlling your time rather than having your time control you.

- Be good to yourself. You cannot always count on those around you to treat you right, but you can make it a habit of treating yourself right.

- Laughter is therapeutic. Use humor to your advantage. Laughing is a great way to relieve tension and alleviate feelings of overwhelm.

- Don't try to be a perfectionist. Strive for excellence – that will be good enough... and will be a significant factor in keeping your emotions at a manageable level

- Listen attentively and carefully. Poor listening habits creates tension in the communication process.

- Open your mind. Opening your mind to all possibilities helps you resist the emotional builders of pessimism.

- Prepare for key events. Preparing mentally, emotionally, and physically for important events helps you to stay calm in those situations where tension tends to be high.

- Establish a regular daily routine. Eat balanced meals and get adequate sleep...both are emotion-reducers.

- Don't sweat the non-essential stuff because most is non-essential stuff.

Chapter Twenty

A HEALTHIER YOU

Those who are good are often separated from
those who are great by their readiness to perform.

In any competitive environment, such as entrepreneurial sales, it is a given that there will come a time when being mentally and physically ready to perform is called into question. Regardless of where your entrepreneurial journey takes you, you must be physically and mentally fit to succeed. How you treat your health now and in the future will become evident at some point.

If you have not been kind to your body or mind, you will be lucky if we don't see negative manifestations prematurely. Your past will weigh on you, reminding you whether you were kind to yourself or failed to take proper care of your body.

The use of Illegal drugs, alcohol, bad eating habits, lack of proper rest and exercise, and other deterrents to good health will eventually take their toll. Sooner or later, the abuse to the body leaves one bankrupt of strength when strength is most needed.

Do you minimize the use of things that harm the body and mind, eroding your health? Over time, these things will diminish the ability to perform effectively and efficiently. However, when you have taken care of your body, you are always in a position to be physically and mentally ready for any action or situation.

Do you have a strong sense of physical care going forward? Do you have any upcoming events that you're looking forward to with anticipation? Do you feel younger than your actual age? Have you taken steps to have the kind of attitude that reduces the risk of degenerative diseases? If so, you are probably adding life to years and years to your life, as well.

> "Attitude plays a crucial role in overall health. It is the rule, not the exception, in physical care. It is not a choice, but a necessity, to maintain quality physical conditioning year-round. A positive and optimistic attitude about your body can make it a healthier reality. Nothing will mean more to your success than being physically, mentally, and emotionally ready to perform to the best of your abilities whenever you are in a competitive entrepreneurial sales situation."
>
> -Dr. Bob Weil

"Take care of your body, you only get one."
-Yogi Berra

"WHAT YOU EAT--YOU ARE"

In the age of fast food, it is often difficult to eat the right food and in the right amount. Willpower takes a back seat when you are hungry and a fast-food restaurant is nearby. There is often a struggle between will and temptation. When temptation takes over, we eat more of the wrong kinds of food. Do all you can to let your *will* lead the way at mealtimes.

Eating right is crucial to achieving long-term success as an entrepreneur. It is essential to be mindful of the food you eat and how you consume it. Changing eating habits is no simple task, but it holds a genuine significance for striving to reach elite status.

It takes mental toughness to change long-time eating patterns. A smart move is to establish a strategy for eliminating bad eating habits. Give these a good trial run:

- STOP TO EAT. When it is time to eat, eat. Drop what you are doing and focus on eating. You will enjoy it more and find that you won't need to eat as much food.

- SIT TO EAT. Eating on the run often leads to grabbing a snack later on. On the go, we are less aware of how much food we consume. Sit at a table to eat, even if your food arrives in a bag.

- DON'T SHOVEL. Slow down and enjoy your food. You will also experience less bloating. Swallowing air can lead to bloating and create gas. The same occurs when you talk with your mouth full. Take in smaller bites, eat slowly, and chew with your mouth closed.

- STOP EATING BEFORE YOU ARE FULL. Put your fork down at the first tinge of fullness. This allows your brain to catch up with eating as you realize you are full before you overeat.

- REDUCE YOUR SNACKS. Do you tend to over-indulge in calorie-laden products between meals? The best rule is to limit snacking. This is important because It keeps the stomach "turned on," leading to the development of a habit of overeating.

- WATCH WHAT YOU SNACK ON. Okay. If you are a "snacker," let your choice of a snack fall within the 10/5/20 rule. This rule establishes that snacks should have no more than 10% fat, 5% carbohydrates, and 20% sugar of daily requirements. Even then, eating snacks continues to evolve around moderation.

- EAT WITH OTHERS. Research shows eating with others tends to slow down your eating behavior. You also take more time to talk and share. As a result, you eat more slowly, which registers more quickly in the brain that you are full.

A great way to avoid overeating is to focus on 'crunch time'. That is the sound we hear as we chew food. It has a ring of 'crunch', doesn't it? The expert opinion is to 'chew like a cow', which is slow and methodical. The "crunch" sound is a cue--if we listen to it--that tends to make us more aware of regulating how much food we intake."

-Dr. Ted Broer

An old proverb, *"Eat the breakfast of a king, the lunch of a knight and the dinner of a pauper."*

HYDRATION

Drink plenty of liquids—even more, if you want to remain hydrated during physical activity. Hydration is crucial for achieving peak performance, maintaining health, and ensuring safety. You can develop various health concerns when you do not consume enough water or replace enough electrolytes to stay properly hydrated.

Staying hydrated each day has these health benefits:
- regulates body temperature…
- helps the heart pump blood more easily…
- keeps other organs functioning correctly…
- improves physical performance…
- maintains body muscle tone…
- assists the brain to work efficiently…
- aids in digestion…
- keeps joints lubricated…
- prevents infections…
- keeps organs functioning properly…
- delivers nutrients to cells…
- helps to prevent issues like headaches
- fights fatigue/prolongs endurance.

This is an awe-inspiring list that highlights the importance of staying hydrated. Be ever cognizant of it.

Many of you consume sweetened beverages, which are not the best option for staying hydrated. According to experts, energy drinks, sodas, vitamin waters, and even excessive fruit juice can do more harm than good in terms of hydration. We probably stepped on a few toes with that bit of information.

Another word of caution: while not typical, it is possible to drink too much water. When a large amount of water is consumed quickly, it can dilute sodium levels. Light-headedness and dizziness are symptoms of too much water too fast. This can also strain the kidneys as they attempt to eliminate the excess fluid from the body. Drink roughly 80 to 108 ounces per day.

SLEEP

Sleep is vital to your overall health and ability to perform effectively in a sales environment. During sleep, your body works to support healthy brain function and advance the growth and development of your physical health.

Getting adequate sleep affects how well you think, react, work, learn, and get along with others. Inadequate rest plays a large role in raising the risk of long-term health problems. Lack of adequate sleep is a significant detriment to quality performance. It can also affect heart, circulatory, respiratory, and immune systems.

How much sleep is enough? Research demonstrates that salespeople need 8 to 10 hours of sleep to maintain a healthy body. If you are deviating from this requirement, consider seeking help in adjusting your sleep pattern. Here are four steps to more incredible sleep habits recommended by the famous Mayo Clinic:

1. **Stick to a sleep schedule**

    Set aside at least eight hours for sleep. Go to bed and get up at the same time every day, including weekends. Being consistent is essential in reinforcing your body's sleep-wake cycle. The absence of regular sleep leads to mental lapses throughout the day.

2. When you have trouble falling asleep.

If you fail to fall asleep within about 20 minutes of going to bed, leave your bedroom and engage in a relaxing activity. Read or listen to soothing music. Then go back to bed when you're tired. Repeat as needed but continue to maintain your regular sleep schedule as best you can.

3. Be careful what you eat and drink late.

Do not go to bed hungry or stuffed. In particular, avoid heavy or large meals within a few hours of bedtime. For example, eat dinner around 6 p.m. Otherwise, discomfort might keep you awake. The stimulating effects of nicotine and caffeine take hours to wear off and can interfere with sleep. Heavy sweets can also affect sleep.

4. Create a restful and peaceful environment

Keep your room calm, cool, dark, and quiet. Exposure to nightlights or daylight might make it more challenging to fall asleep. Avoid using light-emitting screens for prolonged periods just before bedtime. Consider using room-darkening shades, earplugs, a fan, or other devices to create an environment that suits your needs for a good night's sleep.

5. Manage your thoughts

Try to resolve your worries or concerns before going to bed. Jot down what's on your mind; then set it aside for tomorrow. It will give you something to look forward to.

EXERCISE REGULARLY...FOREVER

Participation in some exercise programs is essential, as is exercising regularly. Walking 30 minutes daily is a beneficial form of exercise. Your doctor can help you decide what's best for you.

Just add an exercise program to your daily routine. It will help you last longer and go further daily.

What is worth noting is what happens after you begin a regular exercise program…you get into the habit of moving and grooving. The carryover value of the lessons you learn will serve you well in the future.

One of the most significant benefits of a regular exercise program is its positive impact on maintaining a healthy body. Research indicates that exercise can lead to a more beneficial cardiovascular system. This means the heart can better circulate blood to all body parts, including the brain, improving memory and mental faculties. Exercise also reduces the risk of cancer, high blood pressure, and diabetes, and helps delay the aging process.

Exercise can also improve appearance. It can help us look and feel young throughout our entire lives. Posture can be improved, and muscles become firmer and more toned. The results: You feel better.

It is advisable to consult your doctor before starting an exercise routine you are unfamiliar with.

> *"The only forms of exercise some folks get are jumping to conclusions…running down others…pushing their luck… and sidestepping their responsibilities."*
> -Source unknown

"PAUSE FOR THE CAUSE"

One of the more challenging things for assertive people to do is to "pause for the cause." There are times when we become victims of our circumstances. Events seem to rush us…press us…move us along at a pace that is injurious to emotional and physical health.

Learn the art of doing nothing. Taking a self-restoring timeout is as much about a mental gain as it a physical gain. This "timeout" gives your creative juices a chance to flourish. It provides an opportunity to think through ideas and solutions that are often overlooked amid the daily hustle and bustle. It also gives your body the time to recharge.

The art of doing nothing requires establishing a decompression zone. It provides you with a time and space where you have nothing planned, where there are no deadlines, no active responsibilities, or places to be. Such a zone allows you to regroup and calibrate yourself without the stress of outside influences. This unwind process will enable you to have what you need when it's time to rewind up again.

Sounds simple. But in the execution of a "pause for the cause," it will take every ounce of mental discipline we can muster to bring it about. You may see this downtime as being unproductive because you are inactive, and it may feel uncomfortable at first. However, once you recognize this time is valuable to success, you will approach it with an open mind.

It took me (Lou) to the third quarter of life to truly understand the importance of a daily timeout. Age can definitely bring wisdom. Unfortunately, what I eventually learned could have surely been put to good use much sooner.

I now make sure to take a few minutes every day to kick back and relax. My body and my mind are much better for it.

Life is to be savored. The beauty of "me-time" is that it is precious and rare. For moments like these, you need the perfect pairing of whatever allows you to relax thoroughly. My idea of quality "me-time" is being alone with some great relaxing music. This enables me to get out of my head and body for a moment. The benefits are remarkable.

Please don't minimize the importance of a "pause for the cause," centered around a little "me-time." This is a great way to get a new perspective on you…and a clearer picture of where your life is headed.

Taking a self-restoring time out is as much about mental gain as it is about physical gain. This "timeout" gives creative juices a chance to flourish. It allows you to think through ideas and solutions that are often buried under the hustle and bustle of daily activities. One of the most important things you can learn is how to do nothing and when you should do it.

As I write this, I (Lou) am making plans to participate in the Senior Tennis Tour next year. When I announced this *"bucket-list"* item to those close to me, I heard a ton of negatives. Probably, the most significant negatives were related to my age and health. But age is just a number, isn't it? I am still in great physical shape for my age. So why not go for it, right?

Optimistic thinking leads to optimistic outcomes. Study after study has shown that optimistic people have more energy…make better decisions…are more productive…are less stressed…are happier…live healthier…and live longer than their pessimistic counterparts.

It is no secret that the body was made to use – not abuse. When the body gives out, it takes your positive attitude and desire to perform well with it. That is a certainty.

Chapter Twenty-One

NON-NEGOTIABLE TRAITS FOR ENTREPRENEURIAL SUCCESS

We want to present what we believe are ten non-negotiable traits (in no particular order) that are core standards and principles for anyone associated with entrepreneurship. Entrepreneurs who enthusiastically embrace the traits of Passion, Self-Confidence, Effort, Focus, Pressure Tolerance, Adaptability, Mental Toughness, Courage, Hustle, and Fun are on a course toward enjoying more substantial sales and marketing possibilities.

There is a significant difference between being interested in these traits and being passionate about incorporating them into your sales life. When you are interested in something, you work at it only when convenient. When you are passionate about something, you do it with all your being.

Your primary goal should be to strive to become something exceptional as an entrepreneur. To achieve this worthy goal, you need to proficiently utilize these ten traits in your sales and marketing strategy. You must be willing to learn how to incorporate these valuable attributes into your daily sales routine. These traits can help you attract new business and expand your client base.

PASSION

Passion sparks the desire to do your best and grow your business to levels that far exceed your original expectations. Passion is nurtured from the inside out. It originates in a heart that yearns to ride the winds of a successful adventure. It is the key to developing into the person you want to become. Others may not remember your exact actions, but they will remember the passion you demonstrated. Is your PASS-I-ON worth passing on?

SELF-CONFIDENCE

These wise words set the tone well in this discussion about asking for "Yes." Self-confidence is essential for consistency when making a buying decision.

Many talented entrepreneurs fail to reach their full potential because they lack self-confidence. Significant factors that interfere with self-confidence include low self-esteem, insecurity, an inferiority complex, or general self-doubt.

Building a bright future depends on possessing self-confidence, particularly when seeking a "yes" from a potential customer. Your remarkable capabilities will grow in tandem with your self-confidence. Therefore, conquer this quest for self-confidence to set the stage for fulfilling your potential. How you view yourself will play a crucial role in your future.

If you tend to look at the "negatives" about yourself at the expense of your many "positive" qualities, the points below should interest you in building your self-confidence:

- **Be prepared**. Knowledge management is crucial to developing self-confidence. The more you know, the more comfortable you will be sharing it.

- **Develop a growth mindset**. A great way to get out of a self-deprecating and low self-esteem loop is to think about where you are headed, not where you have been. Focus on what you will do to make progress today.

- **Be excited about what you do.** Being fired up about tackling the challenges you face is vital in building the self-confidence needed to overcome them.

- **Stay active**. You will not acquire self-confidence sitting around waiting for something to happen. You must be actively involved in developing skills and improving overall abilities. Success in expanding your self-confidence level is very much a do-it-yourself project.

- **Speak the winners' language**. Talk to yourself like a winner. The positive affirmations you tell yourself are vital to self-confidence and business longevity. Be a self-coach, not a self-critic.

- **Conduct mental rehearsals**. Visualize in your mind's eye what you will do today to create positive outcomes. When you conduct mental trials and follow up with responsive action, your self-confidence is dramatically enhanced, leading to improved results.

- **Expect the best**. When you mentally believe that something good will happen today, your confidence level will follow that path.

- **Exercise patience.** A deep and abiding confidence in yourself is something that takes time. It must be coaxed in steps. Ultimately, your earnings will result from short, consistent gains.

- **Act the part**. Act out the role until you feel comfortable playing it. Be a beacon of confidence around others. Nothing is more enlightening to others than letting your light shine so brightly that they are compelled to reciprocate. Worth a thought.

- **Associate with successful people**. Spend little time with those who are a haven for negative thoughts. You gain self-confidence by associating with those who encourage you, who help you, and who appreciate that you can succeed in the sales world.

- **Celebrate your successes**. Whether the achievement is small or large, patting yourself on the back is okay.

EFFORT

Effort arises from both physical capacity
and a steadfast and determined desire to succeed.

Why do two entrepreneurs with comparable abilities and skill sets often experience vastly different results? An entrepreneur with only average ability and skills may consistently perform above expectations, while another with exceptional ability regularly falls short of quality results.

A significant part of the answer to this question can be found in their work ethic. Work ethics determine how much effort one puts into turning dreams into reality. It is a core value based on solid determination, durable work, and impeccable diligence. Those with strong, positive work habits tend to get a leg up on others because they work efficiently and wiser.

Effort is an inherent attitude that a person develops about themself and the quality and depth of their work ethic. Individuals with inadequate effort tend to do just enough to get by and will likely eventually see their dreams go up in smoke. Quality application in everything you do can subsequently become a part of your belief system. That's a philosophy that will carry any entrepreneur a long way.

What is your philosophy of effort? Do you possess a high level of intensity in your work patterns? This is one thing that is definitely within your own control. You have complete control over it. Focusing on what you must do to achieve your goals depends on developing the best work habits you can. This is what leads to more positive outcomes and superb overall results.

Those with solid effort are intrinsically motivated to do their best and are rewarded by delivering consistently high results. Through sheer willpower and determination, they place a high value on doing what is expected of them to the best of their ability…then they do more. They continually seek to solve problems and seek opportunities to expand their sales results. Effort is their watchword.

The ladder to sales success is built on the effort you put into your adventure and how it is cultivated through daily use. As someone aptly pointed out, *"Hard work beats talent when talent doesn't work hard."*

It is crucial to your future to understand that performing well can never be regarded as incidental or accidental. It is a direct reflection of your attitude toward employing quality work ethics. Drawing on the intense effort you put in will help you continually develop and grow your business.

The experience of putting in quality effort leads to accomplishing more in less time. This creates more growth opportunities. Buried deep in applying yourself with a strong work ethic is how it speeds up getting to the "good part" faster. Applying yourself more comprehensively and thoroughly will yield more outstanding results. An intense effort may be your number one asset in the larger scheme of things.

FOCUS (ATTENTIVE PRESENCE)

Attention maximizes intentions.

Why is it difficult to be fully attentive to anything? It is likely because the world is full of distractions, which diminishes the ability to provide undivided attention. Quality sales results are directly proportional to being present with customers in a genuine and wholehearted manner. Block out the distractions and provide a willing ear.

It has been said that the quickest way to accomplish many things is to focus on doing only one thing at a time. The vital truth is that directing all your attention and energy toward the individual you are conversing with enables you to perceive them better. Being capable and thorough in acquiring information allows one to relate to that individual on a more profound level.

Learning to concentrate on each person is a skill that can be acquired. It is impossible to force yourself to focus on anything! The ability to concentrate is formulated around the habit of being overly interested in a specific thing. In sales and marketing circles, that one thing is each customer. Focus naturally happens when you want to learn as much as possible about customers and their gateway challenges.

Again, let us emphasize that the key to *"being wherever you are"* mainly depends on your ability to block out the distracting things happening around and within you. When you are focused, you are more apt to focus on one thing—or one person—at a time and prioritize that.

The more you apply the *"focus on one customer at a time"* theme, the deeper your relationships with that customer will be. When your concentration is intense, you refrain from ever considering the possibility that you may not develop a strong relationship with any prospective customer you meet.

Make these thoughts on focusing a part of you:

- It's worth remembering that whatever gets your attention gets you... for wherever your real focus is, that's where your heart should be.

- When you absorb yourself in action, a mistake or setback will not fracture your approach; you will view it as only temporary...and nothing else

- Focus on each situation as it appears. You cannot do everything that needs to be done at once, but you can do the one thing that needs to be done immediately.

- When you focus on the task at hand, you are less sensitive to the "negatives" around you—the kind of things that work against you taking a positive approach toward what you are working on at any given moment.

- Your best chance is where you are right now... for what you might consider "no chance" may well be your only chance to make a sale.

- When you are "always where you are" – whether in front of a customer, in your office, or on the computer— always focused on something that will move you forward.

- Concentrate on your role -- not what others do, or are supposed to do—and initiate the effort to perform your role to the best of your ability.

- *"Those who lose focus -- lose."* You will never perform as capably as possible unless you direct all your energy toward one situation or task.

- To do something different, you must focus on doing something different.

- Focus on today... and make it the best day of your career.

PRESSURE TOLERANCE

There are no pressure situations...only situations
where participants feel or experience pressure.

When right on the brink of asking a prospect to accept an offer, some flinch... retreat..., or lose courage when it is most needed. Why? In our experience, the perception of a critical point in a sale is inherently altered by one of the most notable pressures known to entrepreneurs: pressure.

How effective are you at handling so-called "pressure situations"? Do you match up well with stressful circumstances? How does your body hold up when you face those anxious moments? Does your heart pound more than usual? Does a big lump develop in your throat? Do you have doubts about how to meet the stressful situation head-on and create a desired outcome?

A truism of *"pressure situations"* is that they can either bring out the best in you, or the worst, depending on how you view it and manage the situation. When released inwardly, it has a detrimental impact by producing distinct changes in the body's physiological nature. Notably, the blood vessels constrict, reducing blood flow to the brain and affecting the ability to think clearly. The results are predictable: performance is less than it could be.

Pressure can be a powerful force when directed outward. Those *"pressure situations"* can bring more in-depth meaning to a sales interview. Depending on your face, this may vary from task to task...from situation to situation. But there is a brighter side to the stress produced by pressure situations.

There are several important lessons I (Lou) learned in baseball. They have an application here:

- The season's first contest (sales accounting period) is just as important as the last.

- One game (sale) is never more critical than another game (sale).

- One play (task) is never more essential than another play (task).

- When you focus on what you have been trained to do in every game (sale) situation and every play (task), then no one situation is ever more critical than the next- they are all critical.

- Your number one job when the stakes are high and the rewards are great is to do the one thing you set out to do—satisfy the customer's needs. That is job one. I (Lou) had one job as a pro baseball pitcher: getting every batter out. Every pitch had something at stake.

The word pressure is tossed around a lot—a natural part of the competitive world's vernacular—but your mindset in the future should be that everything that happens during a sale carries the same weight. Your goal is to embrace where you are and visualize performing optimally at what you do at any moment. Easier said than done. However, it can be done with the right mindset.

The ability to thrive under stressful conditions depends entirely on emphasizing doing your best on every sales opportunity. This is the best way to minimize control over your performance in those so-called "pressure situations".

Consider it an honor to experience pressure…it means you are in the midst of doing something important."
-Novak Djokovic

ADAPTABILITY

Marketing and sales are characterized by sudden, unexpected, and sometimes dramatic challenges. Your capacity to rise effectively to meet and confront challenges is crucial in your role as an entrepreneur. A knack for taking a decision-making attitude can often make a significant difference in producing substantial results.

Functioning in a rapidly changing environment requires developing a flexible and adaptable ability to adapt. An adaptive mindset is a conditioned mind that has been systematically trained, focused, concentrated, and tempered to reconcile and cope with the immediate external changes in sales. Adaptive thinking helps you apply sound reasoning to quickly and accurately recognize and perceive the actual reality of sales actions.

Armed with adaptability, you can maintain composure even in the most competitive and pressure-filled situations. Through an adaptive mindset, you learn to avoid extremes and overreactions. Adapting quickly and efficiently minimizes emotional surges during actual game action, providing a stable power source.

Adaptability is a learned behavior. It is an essential factor in your ability to move your future forward. However, it can be challenging to recognize any variation in behavior that challenges a core belief or is inconsistent with past behavior.

Letting go is never easy. Altering how we have done things calls for the highest level of adaptability and change. It will require you to do your best to get into a groove of adaptive behavior. When you do, you display more flexibility in your sales efforts.

Sometimes, the "old ways" are the only ways because that's what you first learned. However, your sales and marketing efforts will be limited until you "let go" of them to create room for something better. Detaching yourself from things that feel comfortable is challenging if you want to expand your horizons.

How you approach changing your "old ways" makes all the difference in whether you are successful. We are discussing creating an adaptive mindset where things improve because you have the fortitude and drive to discover how to improve them.

A simple fact, when the intent is to adapt to new and more constructive ways of doing things, is that you never let go entirely of the past. There will always be something of the past left within you. Every new beginning carries with it a lesson from things you have done. There is always something from the past that can be adapted to the future.

Do you believe there is something better out there than you have ever experienced? If the answer is "Yes," then your ability to adapt and do something different must be done deliberately. Adaptability works best when you are proactive, leveraging the insight that enables you to make needed adjustments reactively. Armed with this kind of foresight, you can develop a diverse arsenal of marketing strategies and tactics that will help unlock the door to future growth.

MENTAL TOUGHNESS

This trait is needed to move from the land of familiarity into the land of promise. There is no light switch to flip to turn on your mental toughness. It is rooted deep within yourself. It is very personal. Mental toughness is more a matter of the heart than the mind. It is the one generational tool that helps you alter your thinking. It has withstood the test of time.

A shortcoming in developing mental toughness is the inability to recognize and appreciate that obstacles and difficulties are essential for personal growth and development of responsibility. Who you want to be and who you are are generally two different things. Mental toughness is at the core of your drive to devise ways to create who you are and what you can do. You cannot succeed significantly without overcoming the challenges that test your mental toughness.

The elements of success are found in your ability to possess mental toughness—it can be readily available when those demanding situations arise. That might require a shift in habits. It is a prelude to a requirement that you rewire and retool the way you think; you may even have to see differently. But when you have a toolbox full of generational wisdom, the necessary adjustments are more easy to make.

In a competitive world, there are always rough patches in your attempt to convince others of your way of thinking, join your cause, or follow your directions. Many varied scenarios affect sales success. One is that it arises from situations where you take the initiative, request an action, and end up being turned down. Mental toughness is a valuable asset in navigating roadblocks.

The gift of mental toughness is that there is no reasonable obstacle you cannot overcome and stay on the course to achieving your dreams. Where others often see enormous challenges in their path, you see opportunity because you have made mental toughness a part of your daily routine.

NOW COURAGE

The opposite of fear is said to be courage. Fear is a mindset. Courage is an action. Courage works from the inside out. It changes how you think, speak, and act. However, it is only worthwhile when applied "now," where it is most needed.

Remedial action is required if you are bogged down in a regimented sales life defined by drudgery, adversity, and stumbling blocks of your own making. Action begins with the traditional trait of courage–or, as we prefer, *now courage*. This is the ability to initiate a solitary act that improves sales, now.

The power of *now* courage is well documented. The fundamental forces that were at work eons ago still operate today. But courage is not an all-encompassing trait. It may be present in one situation but not in another, which is quite common for most of us.

The challenge of *now* courage is the inability to see what is on the other side. You probably know what awaits you when you arrive there. The same *now* courage that got you headed in the right direction is the same *now* courage that will deepen your belief in the fantastic opportunities that exist in your future.

One of the most therapeutic things you can do to establish the *now* courage that will move you beyond any fear is the power of suggestion. You may never know how to function without chaos until you make the mental suggestion to use your faith in yourself to move you beyond any fear.

It is not hard to act when you must... the key is having the now courage to act when nothing is pushing you.

You don't need courage to face what you already know. You need courage to face the uncertainty of the future. Every opportunity carries a kernel of fear, but it also holds the seed of something better within it. Having the *now* courage to discover it is one of the things *now* courage is for.

Success reflects the now courage to create movement and action.

HUSTLE

HUSTLE IS

HUSTLE IS an indirect yet decisive daily movement toward the pursuit of an upward path.

HUSTLE IS doing all that is expected of you–even if no one is watching.

HUSTLE IS staying the course through grit and grime... sweat and tears... bumps and bruises.

HUSTLE IS about having a strong work ethic to tackle any challenge and then approaching it with gusto.

HUSTLE IS doing your best with conditions as you find them, even if you would like to have a different set of conditions.

HUSTLE IS continuing to do something that all around you are certain cannot be done.

HUSTLE IS doing the little things others would not think worth doing... and doing them well.

HUSTLE IS doing the things you must do- when you must do them- to make positive things happen.

HUSTLE IS the condition created when you get desire and enthusiasm moving in the same direction.

HUSTLE IS doing your best, even if no one is watching.

HUSTLE IS racing to fulfill a dream, with no speed limit in pursuing excellence and generating success.

HUSTLE IS in the words of the great coach, Vince Lombardi,"...that moment when you have worked your heart out and lie exhausted on the field of battle -- victorious."

FUN

Surprised? That's right. No fancy title here: Every entrepreneur needs to have fun. Why do something if you fail to enjoy it and have fun at it?

Sales participation can be very intense and demanding, lessening the joy you can receive from involvement. Unless you find something within the experience that revitalizes your spirit and makes you feel great about doing it, you will be hard-pressed to perform at a championship level.

Undoubtedly, the ability to sustain motivation comes from loving what you do and the enjoyment you receive from interacting with others. The drive required to perform any task effectively is more readily accessible through the power generated by interacting with people from all walks of life. Experiencing celebratory occasions and successes enhances the delight and pleasure of selling.

Having fun is vital to success in any sales activity. Here are some essential benefits of this role.

· Provides perspective
· Enhances the ability to adapt
· Enhances interest
· Increases productivity
· Defuses stress

EPILOGUE

We bet you have already taken gigantic steps toward realizing your potential. Knowing that we may have made a small difference in your development journey excites us. What is essential is the great discovery you have made about yourself as we moved through the book together. Genuinely, we believe this is the beginning of a new ending for you. We celebrate with you.

Over these years, we have discovered that the growth opportunities presented to you as an entrepreneur become more prevalent the more actively you create and pursue them. Some of these opportunities arise from experience, some from experimentation, some from examples, some from making mistakes, and some from unexpected places. However, they all come when you are energetic and searching for them.

Now, as you prepare to leave us and ride off from what you are today to seek what you will become tomorrow, the mystery and adventure of the journey are in great hands—your own. Keep learning. Keep applying. Keep hustling. Keep improving. Keep this book close at hand. Whether in sales or life, this book can serve as an authentic reference source for your future. The nature of this book requires the gift of presence. It demands the gift of action. Up to it?

> **That change in your entrepreneurial career you envision that will enhance your future...do it now. Get a running start and jump right on in...and you might just be surprised at the stunning and exciting place where you land.**

THE ENTREPRENEURIAL PROFESSIONAL

Being an entrepreneurial professional is, first and foremost, a commitment to being the best you can be at all times...in all situations.

It is about clearly seeing where you are going —not having a scattered vision.

It's about possessing a well-defined purpose and an intense desire to move beyond average and aspire toward excellence.

It is about having discipline and self-mastery to distance yourself from intolerance and overindulgence.

It's about preparing yourself with an education and acquiring expertise that the amateur fails to pursue.

It is about complete dedication to yourself...your clients... and your company.

It is about being attuned to the desires of those you wish to serve and viewing circumstances from their perspective.

It is about equipping yourself with the discernment to make wise choices and decisions for all concerned parties.

It is about possessing an attitude of service that prompts others to accept your guidance and counseling readily.

Being an entrepreneurial professional is doing your best to make everything around you better.

ABOUT LOU VICKERY...

Lou Vickery is a #1 International Best-Selling author. He has authored twenty-four books on a variety of topics. Lou's work life has been an incredible journey. He has had four distinct careers: professional baseball player, stockbroker with Merrill Lynch, sales trainer /motivational speaker, and a radio and TV talk show host.

Lou is a graduate of Troy University. He attended college in the off-season from pro baseball and took ten years to graduate. Lou is a past member of the Alumni Board of Trustees.

Lou has traveled to every state except Alaska for pro baseball and/or speaking engagements. He has spoken in every city with a population of over 150,000. Thousands of people have participated in his seminars, training, and development sessions. And Lou has seen all the magnificent sights from coast to coast.

Lou has rubbed shoulders with highly successful individuals from diverse backgrounds, including athletes, businessmen, and world leaders. On his Radio and TV shows, Lou hosted guests ranging from U.S. Senators to a Pulitzer Prize winner to a clown.

Lou's brand is A WISE WORD. He is known as *"The Voice of Generational Wisdom."* You can see Lou spreading his wisdom on his YouTube Channel www.youtube.com/@awiseword, or a tennis court.

Lou has been a member of numerous organizations, including the National Speakers Association. He served two terms as President of his hometown, Atmore, AL, Rotary Club, and founded the Atmore Area Hall of Fame.

ABOUT JIM (GYMBEAX) BROWN...

Jim "Gymbeaux" Brown isn't your everyday professional entrepreneur. With a 20-year tenure in the U.S. Coast Guard, specializing in Personnel Administration and Merchant Marine Safety, and over 33 years as a real estate leader—salesman, company owner, broker, manager, team leader, and trainer—he's a powerhouse of experience.

But Jim isn't just about titles. He's a lifelong student, having read over 1,000 books on sales, relationships, team building, and the psychology of selling. He's also written and published more than 1,000 Nuggets for the Noggin, short but insightful articles on sales, management, motivation, and book reviews, found on his blog: www.NuggetsfortheNoggin.com.

A proud alumnus of Bowling Green State University with a focus on Marketing and Advertising, Jim sums up his passion in one statement: *"To help people do what they do and do it better!"*

A man of wisdom, experience, and an unwavering commitment to personal growth—"Gymbeaux" proves that success is a lifelong journey. His self-education continues, and he challenges others to embrace the same mindset. *"I may not always have the answers right away, but I'm confident I can point you in the right direction."* You can reach Jim at TheJimBrown@pm.me.

Jim and his wife Diane have been married for 57 years. They have built a legacy that spans four children, nine grandchildren, and four great-grandchildren.

www.ingramcontent.com/pod-product-compliance
Lightning Source LLC
Chambersburg PA
CBHW060037030426
42334CB00019B/2368